LOVELY LAYER CAKES

PEGGY PORSCHEN

Photography by Georgia Glynn Smith

QUADRILLE

DEDICATION

For Max and Bryn,
with all my love.

Publishing Director Jane O'Shea
Commissioning Editor Lisa Pendreigh
Project Editor Katie Golsby
Creative Director Helen Lewis
Designer Gemma Hayden
Photographer Georgia Glynn Smith
Stylist Rebecca Newport
Production Director Vincent Smith
Production Controller Tom Moore

Props kindly provided by:
Talking Tables www.talkingtables.co.uk
India Jane www.indiajane.co.uk
Jane Means www.janemeans.com
Dotcomgiftshop www.dotcomgiftshop.com
Nina Campbell www.ninacampbell.com
Maids to Measure www.maidstomeasure.com

First published in 2015 by
Quadrille Publishing Ltd
Pentagon House, 52–54 Southwark Street,
London SE1 1UN
www.quadrille.co.uk

Quadrille is an imprint of Hardie Grant
www.hardiegrant.com.au

Text, recipes and cake designs
© 2015 Peggy Porschen
Photography
© 2015 Georgia Glynn Smith
Artwork, design and layout
© 2015 Quadrille Publishing Ltd

British Library Cataloguing-in-Publication Data
A catalogue record for this book is available
from the British Library

ISBN 978 1 84949 729 9

Printed in China

CONTENTS

6 Introduction
8 Basic Tool Kits
9 Top Tips for Baking the Perfect Sponge
10 Basic Fillings and Frostings
14 Raspberry Kiss Cake
18 Blueberry and Buttermilk Cake
22 Milk and Honey Cake
26 Rose and Pistachio Cake
30 Snowball Cake
34 Salted Caramel Cake
40 Vanilla Cloud Cake
46 Cookies and Cream Cake
50 Lemon, Raspberry, and Rose Cake
54 French Violet Cake
60 Red Velvet Cake
64 Toffee Apple Cake
68 Black and White Devil's Food Cake
72 Passion Fruit and Mascarpone Cake
76 Chocolate Praline Truffle Cake
82 Maple and Walnut Cake

86 Tiramisu Cake
92 Citrus Cake
96 Berry Basket Cake
100 Gingerbread Cake
104 Sugar Plum Cake
110 Spiced Pumpkin Cake
114 Neapolitan Cake
118 Black Forest Cake
122 Cheeky Monkey Cake
126 Strawberry and Champagne Cake
130 S'mores Cake
136 Mad Hatter's Checkerboard Cake
142 Peach and Almond Torte
146 Piña Colada Cake
150 Layering Technique
152 Masking Technique
154 Piping Techniques
156 Index
158 Suppliers
159 Acknowledgments

INTRODUCTION

Lovely Layer Cakes is a book about two things I truly love: baking and creating beautiful, delicious cakes. I have loved cakes for as long as I can remember. I love looking at them, smelling them, eating them and, most of all, I love making them.

My love for cakes goes back to my very early childhood. Although people say that one's memories only go back to about the age of four, I still remember the moment of my very first birthday when my mom presented me with a lovely buttercream cake, covered in marzipan, with little sugar animals on top. (I have the photograph to prove it.) From that point, my birthday cake was the highlight of my year and, on my birthday, I always cared more about the cake than about my presents. I love how a cake brings people together around a table. A cake means a gathering of family and friends, it means happy moments and memories. So, what better way to celebrate a festive occasion than with a wonderful cake?

I was inspired to write *Lovely Layer Cakes* for all those reasons, and to combine creativity with delicious baking. At my home in Germany we have a similar saying to the English expression, "You first eat with your eyes." I have always cared about how a cake looks just as much as how it tastes. I meet a lot of people through my work who say that they can bake a delicious cake but, when it comes to the finishing touches, they struggle. The recipes in this book are about combining the most wonderful sponge cakes with delectable cake fillings and toppings that taste as good as they look. Some of the recipes are all-time classics, such as the Victoria sponge that is used as the base for the Citrus Cake (pages 92 to 95) and the chocolate ganache that covers the Salted Caramel Cake (pages 34 to 39), but I am always searching for the perfect version of any recipe so I often revisit them time and time again. Sometimes I use a classic recipe as the basis for a new flavor combination and add a new twist, such as in the Blueberry and Buttermilk Cake (pages 18 to 21).

Before you start making any of the recipes in this book, I recommend that you carefully read through my top tips for baking the perfect sponge. If you follow the simple advice given here, you should avoid the disappointment of opening the oven to find that your sponge hasn't risen, or is burned. The section on basic fillings and frostings offers a selection of recipes for buttercreams, frostings, ganache, and sugar syrup, which you can flavor to your own taste and combine with the cake base of your choice. Toward the end of the book is a guide to layering and masking your cakes, with detailed step-by-step photography; I hope you will find this helpful, and that the advice given enables you to produce cakes that not only taste amazing, but also look worthy of the occasions that they are made for. For pretty finishing touches, there is a display of the different piping techniques that are used in the recipes. Finally, to help you to achieve simple yet effective cake decoration, I have designed two easy-to-use cake stencils that you will find tucked into the back of this book.

I hope you will enjoy baking *Lovely Layer Cakes* as much as I do.

Enjoy.

BASIC TOOL KITS

THE LISTS BELOW INCLUDE ALL THE TOOLS YOU WILL NEED TO CREATE THE LAYER CAKES IN THIS BOOK. IF YOU ARE ALREADY A KEEN HOME BAKER, YOU WILL PROBABLY HAVE IN YOUR KITCHEN MOST OF THE ITEMS LISTED IN THE BAKING TOOL KIT. THE LAYERING TOOLS ARE MORE SPECIFIC AND ARE A WORTHWHILE INVESTMENT TO ACHIEVE PERFECT RESULTS IF YOU WOULD LIKE TO TAKE YOUR CAKE-MAKING SKILLS TO THE NEXT LEVEL, AND THEY SHOULD SERVE YOU WELL FOR MANY YEARS TO COME.

BAKING TOOL KIT

1. Electric mixer with whisk and paddle attachment
2. Selection of cake pans and baking sheets
3. Rubber spatula
4. Selection of bowls and pitchers
5. Selection of large and small fine strainers
6. Kitchen scale
7. Wax paper
8. Step palette knife
9. Pastry brush
10. Scissors
11. Wire rack
12. Small kitchen knife
13. Whisk
14. Oven mitts
15. Measuring spoons
16. Plastic wrap
17. Oil spray

LAYERING TOOL KIT

1. Long serrated knife or cake leveler
2. Ruler that measures in inches
3. Cake boards in various shapes and sizes
4. Small, medium, and large palette knives
5. Nonslip turntable
6. Metal cake disk
7. Metal side scraper
8. Selection of pastry bags (such as paper, plastic, and textile with screw attachment)
9. Assortment of metal piping tips (different sizes of round and star tips)

Tucked inside the back cover of this book, you will find two food-safe stencils for decorating your layer cakes. For instructions on how to use these stencils, turn to pages 57 to 8. Made from food-safe plastic, these stencils can be used repeatedly. After each use, wash and dry the stencils. Wash the stencils by hand in warm soapy water and thoroughly dry them by laying them flat between sheets of paper towels and patting gently.

TOP TIPS FOR BAKING THE PERFECT SPONGE

BAKING MAY BE A SCIENCE BUT, IF YOU FOLLOW A FEW SIMPLE RULES, YOU WILL ACHIEVE CONSISTENTLY GOOD RESULTS AND EVENLY BAKED CAKES. HERE, I HAVE LISTED THE TIPS THAT I SWEAR BY WHEN IT COMES TO MAKING THE PERFECT SPONGE.

INGREDIENTS

1. Using good-quality ingredients really makes a difference, not only to the flavor but also to the bake. Always use free-range eggs, butter rather than margarine, and genuine spices, zests, and extracts (not essences) where possible.

2. Unless otherwise stated, the eggs and butter should be the same temperature (room temperature is best) to prevent curdling, which will result in a low rise. For the same reason, always add the eggs gradually and beat well after each addition, until combined.

3. Bring the butter to room temperature before use, then cream together with the sugar until light and fluffy.

4. If a cake contains chopped fruits, cookies, or nuts, gently fold them in at the very end. To keep them from sinking to the bottom of the cake during baking, toss them with about one-quarter of the dry ingredients and gently fold them into the batter.

5. It is important to use soft cake flour to achieve a good texture—don't be tempted to use a strong flour, such as bread flour, as it will make the sponge tough.

MEASUREMENTS

1. Use digital kitchen scale and cups as opposed to traditional weighing scale, as they are much more precise. Weigh out your ingredients as accurately as possible and scrape out the bowls thoroughly.

2. Always use measuring spoons rather than a teaspoon or tablespoon from the cutlery drawer. Unless the recipe states otherwise, always level the top of the spoon with a knife.

3. Some of the recipes use medium eggs, some extra-large—on average, the cracked weight of a medium egg is 1¾ oz (50 g) and for an extra-large egg it is 2¼ oz (60 g). If you have eggs of unequal sizes, calculate the total weight of egg needed, crack the eggs and weigh out the quantity required.

CAKE PANS

1. For light, evenly browned cakes, use shiny cake pans rather than dark or discolored ones, as these will overbrown or even burn the cake.

2. I prefer to use a shallow sandwich pan for each layer (mine are 1½ in/4 cm deep), rather than one deep pan for the whole cake, as shallow sponges bake quicker, more evenly, and rise better.

3. Spray the bottom and sides of the cake pan with oil and line the bottom with a disk of wax paper.

4. Always spread the cake batter so it's a little higher around the edges than in the middle. This will prevent the sponge from "erupting" in the center.

5. Once filled, place the cake pans in a preheated oven as soon as possible; otherwise, the raising agent in the cake batter could lose its effect.

6. After baking, remove the sponges from the oven and let rest for 10 minutes. While still in the pan, brush with sugar syrup, using a pastry brush, and let rest for another 20 to 30 minutes until cool enough to handle. Run a small kitchen knife around the edges of the pans to release the sponges, then transfer to a wire rack and let cool completely.

TIMING AND TEMPERATURES

1. Use any given timings and temperatures as a guide only, as ovens can vary greatly in their accuracy. The temperatures stated are for conventional ovens, so you will need to reduce the temperature by 25°F (10°C) if using a fan-assisted oven.

2. A lot of domestic ovens have hot spots. If this applies to your oven, turn the cake pans halfway through cooking to ensure even baking.

BASIC FILLINGS AND FROSTINGS

THE CAKE FILLINGS AND FROSTINGS GIVEN HERE ARE USED THROUGHOUT THE BOOK. IT IS IMPORTANT TO ENSURE THAT YOU FOLLOW THE TIME PLAN GIVEN IN EACH CAKE RECIPE, SO THAT YOUR FILLING OR FROSTING IS THE REQUIRED TEMPERATURE AND CONSISTENCY AT THE TIME YOU NEED IT. THIS IS ESSENTIAL, TO GUARANTEE THAT THE CAKE HOLDS ITS SHAPE AND THAT THE OUTER COAT LOOKS SMOOTH AND NEAT. AS A GENERAL RULE, THE HEAVIER AND DENSER THE SPONGE, THE HEAVIER AND DENSER THE FROSTING SHOULD BE. HOWEVER, MY ADVICE IS TO EXPERIMENT AND USE WHATEVER WORKS BEST FOR YOU.

ENGLISH BUTTERCREAM

Making English buttercream is very straightforward; all you need is a good electric mixer. Made using just butter and powdered sugar, the key to making it light and fluffy is beating it to incorporate as much air as possible. English buttercream doesn't split and holds up well, making it ideal for piped designs such as scrolls and rosettes. To make the buttercream stiffer—for example, on warm summer days—you can increase the amount of sugar up to double the amount of butter.

Makes 14 oz (400 g) English buttercream
⅞ cup (200 g) unsalted butter, softened
1⅔ cups (200 g) powdered sugar, sifted
A pinch of salt

Place the butter, sugar, salt, and any flavoring in the bowl of an electric mixer and, using a paddle attachment, beat at medium speed until light and fluffy.

If not using immediately, store the buttercream in a sealed container in the refrigerator and bring back to room temperature before use. It will keep for up to 2 weeks.

MERINGUE BUTTERCREAM

Meringue buttercream is very light and smooth with a relatively pale color. It is more delicate than English buttercream and suits lighter sponges, such as chiffon cake. It can split easily if overworked or mixed with acidic ingredients or those with a high fat content, such as ganache. Always add other flavors very carefully, folding them through gently. Should the buttercream split, you can bring it back by whipping it at high speed (unless it is mixed with a filling containing a high fat content). Cakes filled with meringue buttercream should always be stored in the refrigerator because of the egg content.

Makes enough to layer one 6-in (15-cm) cake
1⅓ cups (270 g) superfine sugar
¼ cup (67 ml) water
4¾ oz (135 g) egg whites, fresh or pasteurized
1½ cups (330 g) butter, softened

Place the sugar and water in a small saucepan over medium-high heat and bring to a rapid boil.

Place the egg whites in the bowl of an electric mixer and whip at low speed, using the whisk attachment, until frothy.

When the sugar syrup reaches 250°F (121°C), with the mixer running, pour it directly over the meringue in a thin, steady stream. Take care not to pour any of the syrup onto the whisk or the sides of the bowl.

Whip the meringue until cool to the touch; this could take several minutes. With the mixer running, add the butter 2 Tbsp at a time. Keep beating until the buttercream is completely smooth and spreadable, then fold in any additional flavorings.

Meringue buttercream will keep for up to 1 week in the refrigerator.

CREAM-CHEESE FROSTING

This is a scrumptious recipe that is perfectly coupled with many American-style cakes, such as the iconic Red Velvet Cake or Black and White Devil's Food Cake (pages 60 and 68). It is softer than buttercream and needs to be refrigerated until serving.

Makes 2¾-lb (1.125-kg) cream-cheese frosting
1 cup (250 g) whole cream cheese, slightly softened
Generous 1 cup (250 g) unsalted butter, softened
5¼ cups (625 g) powdered sugar, sifted

Place the cream cheese in a bowl and beat until smooth and creamy using an electric mixer.

Place the butter and a third of the sugar in a separate bowl and cream until very pale and fluffy. Add another third of the sugar and repeat.

Add the remaining sugar and beat again, scraping the sides of the bowl to ensure no lumps remain. Add the cream cheese, a little at a time, and mix at low speed until combined.

Chill until firm enough to spread or pipe.

Cream-cheese frosting will keep for up to 2 weeks in the refrigerator.

MASCARPONE FROSTING

This is a rich cake filling with a creamy texture. You must let it set properly before use, otherwise it won't hold up.

Makes 2¼-lb (1-kg) mascarpone frosting
⅞ cup (200 g) unsalted butter, softened
Scant 4¼ cups (500 g) powdered sugar, sifted
1⅓ cups (300 g) mascarpone, slightly softened

Place the butter and half of the sugar in the bowl of an electric mixer and cream together at high speed until very pale and fluffy.

Add the remaining sugar with the mascarpone and beat at medium-high speed, scraping down the sides of the bowl to ensure no lumps remain.

Beat until the mixture is smooth, but do not overbeat or the mixture will become runny. If necessary, chill until firm enough to pipe.

Chill for several hours until set completely.

Mascarpone frosting will keep for up to 2 weeks in the refrigerator.

CHOCOLATE GANACHE

This is a great basic ganache recipe with slightly less cream than chocolate, which allows it to set to just the right consistency for layering and masking cakes. The glucose adds a beautiful sheen, so it makes an ideal shiny chocolate glaze. For a perfect spreadable texture, let the ganache set slowly at room temperature.

Makes about 14 oz (400 g) chocolate ganache
Scant 1 ¼ cups (200 g) semisweet Belgian chocolate drops (53% cocoa solids)
⅝ cup (150 ml) whipping cream
1 Tbsp (20 g) glucose

Place the chocolate drops in a deep bowl.

Pour the cream and glucose into a deep saucepan and bring to a simmer.

Pour the cream over the chocolate drops and whisk gently until the chocolate has melted and the mixture is smooth.

Let cool until just setting, before use. The ganache can be stored in an airtight container covered with plastic wrap, and will keep for up to 2 weeks at room temperature.

SUGAR SYRUP

If you bake regularly at home, it's a good idea to keep a supply of simple sugar syrup in the refrigerator. I swear by it, as I use it to add moisture and flavor to most of my cakes. Brushing the top of a sponge with syrup just after baking prevents it from forming a dry, hard crust than can spoil the cake. Doing this while the sponge is still warm allows the syrup to absorb more quickly than if the sponge has cooled. For flavored syrup, infuse the syrup with the flavoring as early as possible before use, to let the flavors develop fully.

Makes about ⅞ cup (200 ml) sugar syrup
⅝ cup (150 ml) water
¾ cup (150 g) sugar

Place the water and sugar in a saucepan, stir well, and bring to a boil. Let it cool down.

When lukewarm, add the flavorings. Store the sugar syrup in the refrigerator if not using immediately. It will keep for up to 1 month.

RASPBERRY KISS CAKE

IF YOU WANT TO SAY IT WITH A CAKE, THEN THIS IS THE ONE FOR YOU. NOT ONLY IS IT MADE WITH LOVE, BUT IT ALSO TASTES TANTALIZINGLY SWEET AND SCRUMPTIOUS. THE COMBINATION OF FRESH RASPBERRIES AND BITTERSWEET MELT-IN-THE-MOUTH CHOCOLATE IS A MATCH MADE IN HEAVEN. EVER WONDERED WHAT TO GIVE YOUR SWEETHEART FOR VALENTINE'S DAY? LOOK NO FURTHER.

INGREDIENTS

For the chocolate sponge
1 cup (250 ml) sunflower oil
14 extra-large eggs, separated
4 tsp vanilla extract
3¾ cups (750 g) packed light brown sugar
1⅔ cups (400 ml) water
1 cup (100 g) unsweetened cocoa powder
5 cups (600 g) all-purpose flour
2 tsp baking soda
1 tsp salt

For the chocolate ganache
2¼ cups (400 g) semisweet Belgian chocolate
Drops (53% cocoa solids)
1¼ cups (300 ml) whipping cream
1½ Tbsp (40 g) glucose

For the meringue buttercream
2¾ cups (540 g) superfine sugar
½ cup (135 ml) water
9½oz (270 g) egg whites
3 cups (660 g) butter

For the decoration
2 to 3 cartons of fresh raspberries

EQUIPMENT

Baking tool kit (see page 8)
Layering tool kit (see page 8)
Three 8-in (20-cm) shallow heart-shaped cake pans
(or one deep pan—you will need to increase the baking
time, then cut the sponge into 3 layers)
Pastry bag
Sugar thermometer

Makes one 8-in (20-cm) heart-shaped cake, serving 10 to 12 generous slices.

METHOD
Make the sponge one day ahead.

TO MAKE THE CHOCOLATE SPONGE
Preheat the oven to 325°F (160°C).

Line three 8-in (20-cm) heart-shaped cake pans with oil spray and wax paper.

In a large bowl, using an electric mixer, blend the oil, egg yolks, vanilla extract, light brown sugar, and water until well combined.

Sift the cocoa, flour, baking soda, and salt and gently fold into the mixture.

In a separate bowl, using an electric mixer, whisk the egg whites until they form stiff peaks. Fold into the batter and mix until everything is well combined.

Gently pour the batter into the prepared pans and bake for 20 to 25 minutes. The sponges are cooked when they spring back to the touch and the sides are coming away from the edges of the pans. Alternatively, insert a knife into the middle of the sponge; if it is cooked, the knife will come out clean.

Once the sponges are baked, remove from the oven and let them rest for about 10 minutes.

Once just warm, run a knife all the way around the sides of the pans, transfer the sponges to a wire rack, and let cool completely.

Wrap the cooled sponges in plastic wrap and let them rest overnight at room temperature. This will ensure that all the moisture is sealed and the sponges are the perfect firm texture for trimming and layering.

TO MAKE THE CHOCOLATE GANACHE
Please follow the instructions on page 13 using the amounts given on page 14.

TO MAKE THE MERINGUE BUTTERCREAM
Please follow the instructions on page 10 using the amounts given on page 14.

TO MAKE THE CHOCOLATE BUTTERCREAM
Check that the chocolate ganache and meringue buttercream are the same temperature and texture, then gently fold 1¼ lb (600 g) ganache into 1¼ lb (600 g) buttercream. Take care not to overwork, as the mixture can split easily.

TO ASSEMBLE THE CAKE
Trim the sponges (page 150), then spread a thin covering of the chocolate buttercream onto the top of each layer.

Put some chocolate buttercream into a pastry bag and pipe a small amount into each raspberry.

Arrange the raspberries over one of the cake layers and pipe some more buttercream in between the raspberries until you have a level surface. Place the next sponge layer on top.

Add another layer of raspberries and chocolate buttercream, as above, then position the final sponge layer on the top.

Place the cake on a turntable and mask the top and sides of the cake with the remaining chocolate buttercream, following the instructions on pages 152 to 153.

TO DECORATE
Decorate the top of the cake with a generous covering of fresh raspberries.

Store the cake in the refrigerator if not serving immediately, and serve at room temperature. Keep away from heat or direct sunlight. This cake will keep for about 3 days.

BLUEBERRY AND BUTTERMILK CAKE

I CALL THIS CAKE A CROWD PLEASER BECAUSE IT TASTES SO YUMMY, GOOEY, AND CREAMY; IT ALMOST REMINDS ME OF A MILK SHAKE. YOU COULD EAT IT AT ANY TIME OF THE DAY, EVEN FOR BREAKFAST.

INGREDIENTS

For the buttermilk sponge
½ cup (105 g) butter
1⅓ cups (275 g) superfine sugar
½ tsp vanilla extract
2 eggs
2 cups (250 g) all-purpose flour, sifted
A pinch of salt
1 cup (250 g) buttermilk
1 tsp baking soda
1¼ tsp white wine vinegar
1⅓ cups (200 g) blueberries
2 Tbsp all-purpose flour

For the vanilla syrup
⅝ cup (150 ml) water
¾ cup (150 g) superfine sugar
1 Tbsp vanilla extract

For the vanilla frosting
1 cup (250 g) whole cream cheese, softened slightly
Generous 1 cup (250 g) unsalted butter, softened
5¼ cups (625 g) powdered sugar, sifted
1 Tbsp vanilla extract
Blueberry jam (for layering)

For the decoration
1 Tbsp blueberries
Fresh mint leaves (optional)

EQUIPMENT

Baking tool kit (see page 8)
Layering tool kit (see page 8)
Three 6-in (15-cm) sandwich pans
Patterned side scraper
Pastry bag
Round piping tip no. 3

Makes one 6-in (15-cm) cake, serving 8 generous slices.

METHOD

Make the sponge one day ahead.

TO MAKE THE BUTTERMILK SPONGE
Preheat the oven to 344°F (170°C).

Line three 6-in (15-cm) sandwich pans with oil spray and wax paper.

Place the butter, superfine sugar, and vanilla in an electric mixer and, using the paddle, beat at medium-high speed until the mixture is pale and fluffy.

Beat the eggs lightly in a separate bowl or pitcher, then slowly pour into the butter mixture with the paddle beating at medium speed. If it starts to curdle, add 1 Tbsp flour to bring it back together.

Once the butter, sugar, and eggs are combined, sift the 2 cups (250 g) of flour and salt into a bowl and add a little to the mixture, followed by a little of the buttermilk, beating at low speed. Repeat until all the dry ingredients and buttermilk have been added and are just combined.

Stir the baking soda into the vinegar and quickly add to the mixture.

Using a rubber spatula, fold through the batter to make sure everything is well combined.

Mix the blueberries with the remaining 2 Tbsp of flour, then gently fold into the cake batter.

Transfer the batter to the lined pans and carefully spread toward the edges with a step palette knife. The mixture should be high around the edges and dipped down in the center, to ensure an even bake and level height.

Bake for 20 to 25 minutes. The sponge is cooked if it springs back when touched and the sides are coming away from the edges of the pan. Alternatively, insert a clean knife into the middle of the sponge; if it is cooked, the knife will come out clean.

While the sponges are baking, make a sugar syrup following the instructions on page 13 and flavor with vanilla extract.

Once the sponges are baked, remove from the oven and let rest for about 10 minutes. Brush the tops of the sponges with vanilla syrup (setting aside some for the assembling stage and storing it in the refrigerator overnight).

Once just warm, run a knife all the way around the sides of the pans, remove the sponges, and let cool completely on a wire rack.

Once cool, wrap the sponges in plastic wrap and let them rest overnight at room temperature. This will ensure that all the moisture is sealed and the sponges firm up to the perfect texture for trimming and layering.

TO MAKE THE VANILLA FROSTING
Make a cream-cheese frosting following the instructions on page 12 and add the vanilla extract.

Chill for at least 2 hours, or until set.

TO ASSEMBLE THE CAKE
Trim the three sponge layers, soak the tops with more vanilla syrup, and sandwich together using the blueberry jam for one layer and some of the vanilla frosting for the other. For instructions on how to trim and layer your cake, see pages 150 to 151.

Use vanilla frosting to mask the top and sides of the cake. See the guide to masking on pages 152 to 153. Chill for at least 1 hour (depending on the temperature of your refrigerator).

TO DECORATE
Mask the cake again, with a generous layer of vanilla frosting, and use a side scraper with a patterned edge to go around the side of the cake. Chill again until set.

Fill a small pastry bag with the remaining vanilla frosting and pipe a loop pattern around the edge of the cake (page 154).

Decorate the top of the cake with a small cluster of fresh blueberries and mint leaves.

If stored in the refrigerator, this cake will last for up to 5 days; however, it will taste at its best for the first 3 days. Serve at room temperature.

MILK AND HONEY CAKE

THIS CAKE WILL BRING BACK CHILDHOOD MEMORIES AND EVOKE FEELINGS OF COMFORT AND HAPPINESS. IT TASTES EXACTLY AS ITS NAME SUGGESTS AND IS THE PERFECT CAKE FOR KIDS—BUT GROWN-UPS WILL LIKE IT TOO.

INGREDIENTS

For the honeycomb
1 Tbsp (20 g) honey
1 Tbsp (25 g) glucose
½ cup (100 g) superfine sugar
2½ Tbsp (40 ml) water
1 tsp baking soda

For the buttermilk sponge
9 egg whites
1¼ cups (250 g) superfine sugar
3½ Tbsp (50 ml) vanilla extract
2¾ cups (335 g) all-purpose flour
1½ Tbsp baking powder
A pinch of salt
4 egg yolks
¾ cup (175 ml) buttermilk
2¾ oz (75 g) honeycomb (see above)

For the honey syrup
⅝ cup (150 ml) water
¾ cup (150 g) superfine sugar
2 Tbsp honey

For the honey frosting
1 cup (250 g) whole cream cheese, softened slightly
Generous 1 cup (250 g) unsalted butter, softened
5¼ cups (625 g) powdered sugar, sifted
4 Tbsp honey

For the decoration
A small amount of marzipan or sugar paste
Edible gold luster (powder or spray)

EQUIPMENT

Baking tool kit (see page 8)
Layering tool kit (see page 8)
Rimmed baking sheet
Sugar thermometer
Three 6-in (15-cm) shallow round sandwich pans
Bee silicon mold (see page 156)
Soft artist brush

Makes one 6-in (15-cm) cake, serving 8 generous slices.

METHOD

Make the honeycomb a couple of hours before baking and store in an airtight container. Bake the sponge one day before assembling.

TO MAKE THE HONEYCOMB

Line a rimmed baking sheet with wax paper and cover with oil spray.

Place the honey, glucose, superfine sugar, and water in a large saucepan and bring to a boil.

Let the mixture reach 302°F (150°C), then carefully remove the saucepan from the heat.

Using a whisk, fold in the baking soda, then gently pour onto the prepared baking sheet. Do not spread out the mixture with a spatula or palette knife as it will knock out the air bubbles. Instead, pour it evenly over the sheet.

Let harden for at least 30 minutes. Once cool, break two-thirds of the honeycomb into small pieces and cover the remainder with plastic wrap to protect it from absorbing moisture from the air.

TO MAKE THE BUTTERMILK SPONGE

Preheat the oven to 344°F (170°C).

Line three 6-in (15-cm) sandwich pans with oil spray and wax paper.

Separate the eggs. Put the egg whites in an electric mixer and, using a whisk attachment, whip at high speed until they form soft peaks. Gradually add the sugar and vanillla extract, then beat until stiff and glossy.

Sift the flour, baking powder, and salt into a bowl. Using a paddle attachment, mix the egg white mixture at low speed, incorporating the egg yolks one at a time. Keeping the mixer on low setting, add a third of the sifted dry ingredients to the egg mixture, followed by a third of the buttermilk. Repeat until everything is well incorporated.

Fold in the honeycomb (there should be about a third left for decoration) and gently spoon the batter into the prepared pans. Bake for 20 to 25 minutes or until the cakes spring back when gently prodded and a skewer comes out clean.

Once the sponges are baked, remove from the oven and let cool in the pans for about 10 minutes.

Run a knife all the way around the sides of the pans, remove the sponges, and let cool completely on a wire rack.

Wrap the sponges in plastic wrap and let rest overnight at room temperature. This will ensure that all the moisture is sealed and that the sponges are the perfect texture for trimming and layering.

TO MAKE THE HONEY SYRUP

Make some sugar syrup, following the instructions on page 13. While still warm, add the honey and mix well.

TO MAKE THE HONEY FROSTING

Make some cream-cheese frosting, following the instructions on page 12.

Gently fold in the honey and let chill for at least 2 hours.

TO ASSEMBLE THE CAKE

Trim the three sponge layers and sandwich them together, adding honey frosting and honey syrup between the layers. For instructions, see pages 150 to 151.

Mask the top and sides of the cake with honey frosting. For masking tips, see pages 152 to 153.

TO DECORATE

Make a marzipan or sugar bee using the silicon mold.

Brush the bee with gold luster and let it dry.

Brush or spray the remaining honeycomb pieces with gold luster and then break into small pieces, sprinkle them on top of the cake. Do this at the last minute, as the honeycomb will start to melt once it's in touch with the frosting.

Press the bee onto the edge of the cake and serve.

This cake has a shelf life of up to 5 days if stored in the refrigerator; however, the honeycomb will start to melt after one day of exposure to air and humidity.

ROSE AND PISTACHIO CAKE

THIS IS A MOIST CAKE WITH A NUTTY TEXTURE AND A SUBTLE NOTE OF ROSE.
I DECORATED IT WITH A CONTEMPORARY STENCIL DESIGN, BUT YOU COULD SPRINKLE
OVER FRESH ROSE PETALS AND SERVE IT FOR A SPECIAL OCCASION
OR AS AN INDULGENT DESSERT.

INGREDIENTS

For the pistachio sponge
⅞ cup (200 g) butter
1 cup (200 g) superfine sugar
2 Tbsp pistachio paste
4 eggs
⅔ cup (100 g) pistachios, toasted,
and finely ground
1⅔ cups (200 g) self-rising flour
A pinch of salt

For the sugar syrup
⅝ cup (150 ml) water
¾ cup (150 g) superfine sugar

For the rose buttercream
1⅓ cups (270 g) superfine sugar
¼ cup (67 ml) water
1½ cups (330 g) butter
4¾ oz (135 g) egg whites
2 Tbsp rose water, or to taste
Pink food color

For the sugar dust
5 Tbsp powdered sugar
½ tsp edible green dust

EQUIPMENT

Baking tool kit (see page 8)
Layering tool kit (see page 8)
Three 6-in (15-cm) round sandwich pans
Floral scroll cake stencil (I used a stencil
from my own sugarcraft collection, but
others are available online)
Small plastic sandwich bag

Makes one 6-in (15-cm) cake, serving 8 generous slices.

METHOD
Make the sponge one day ahead.

TO MAKE THE PISTACHIO SPONGE
Preheat the oven to 347°F (175°C).

Line three 6-in (15-cm) sandwich pans with oil spray and wax paper.

Place the butter, superfine sugar, and pistachio paste in an electric mixer and, using the paddle, beat at medium-high speed until pale and fluffy.

Lightly beat the eggs in a separate bowl or pitcher and, with the mixer on medium speed, slowly pour into the butter mixture. Add the ground pistachios and beat until combined.

Sift the flour and salt together and gently fold into the mixture.

Transfer the batter to the lined pans and gently spread out toward the edges with a step palette knife.

Bake for 20 to 25 minutes. The sponges are cooked when they spring back to the touch and the sides are coming away from the edges of the pan. To double-check, you could insert a clean knife into the middle of the sponge; if it is cooked, the knife will come out clean.

While the sponges are in the oven, make the sugar syrup following the instructions on page 13.

When they are baked, remove the sponges from the oven and let rest for about 10 minutes. Brush the tops of the sponges with syrup (setting aside some for the assembling stage and storing it in the refrigerator overnight).

Run a knife all the way around the sides of the pans, remove the sponges, and let cool completely on a wire rack.

Wrap the sponges in plastic wrap and let rest overnight at room temperature. This will seal in all the moisture and ensure that the sponges are nice and firm, ready for trimming and layering.

TO MAKE THE ROSE MERINGUE BUTTERCREAM
Make some meringue buttercream following the instructions on page 10.

Add the rose water according to taste and a little pink food color, and mix well. Be careful not to overwork the mixture as it can split.

TO MAKE THE SUGAR DUST
Put the powdered sugar and edible green dust inside a small plastic bag and mix together until well combined.

TO ASSEMBLE THE CAKE
Trim the three sponges and soak with the sugar syrup. Sandwich together using the rose meringue buttercream. See pages 150 to 151 for instructions on how to trim and layer the cake.

Mask the top and sides of the cake using the remaining rose meringue buttercream (pages 152 to 153). Chill the cake again.

TO DECORATE
When the final layer of buttercream is set and cold, position the floral stencil on the top of the cake so that it overhangs one side of the cake. (If the buttercream isn't quite set, the stencil could get stuck and leave a mark when you lift it off.) Sprinkle the sugar dust over the stencil, ensuring that all the cutouts are well coated. Carefully lift the stencil and place it on the other side of the cake, then dust again.

Store the cake in the refrigerator if not serving immediately, and serve at room temperature. Keep away from heat or direct sunlight. The cake tastes best if consumed within 3 days of baking, but can last for up to 1 week if stored in the refrigerator.

SNOWBALL CAKE

THIS IS A VERY LIGHT, YET INDULGENT, CAKE WITH A CREAMY COCONUT TEXTURE AND A NUTTY TOASTED-ALMOND SPONGE.

INGREDIENTS

For the almond sponge
3 extra-large eggs, separated
1 tsp vanilla extract
½ cup (110 g) superfine sugar
A pinch of salt
¼ cup plus 2 Tbsp (45 g) cornstarch
½ tsp baking powder
1 cup (90 g) ground almonds

For the vanilla syrup
⅝ cup (150 ml) water
¾ cup (150 g) sugar
1 tsp vanilla extract (or to taste)

For the coconut meringue buttercream
1⅓ cups (270 g) superfine sugar
¼ cup (67 ml) water
4¾ oz (135 g) egg whites
1½ cups (330 g) butter
½ oz (15 g) organic creamed coconut

For the decoration
Dry unsweetened coconut

EQUIPMENT

Baking tool kit (see page 8)
Layering tool kit (see page 8)
Three 6-in (15-cm) shallow round sandwich pans

Makes one 6-in (15-cm) cake, serving 8 generous slices.

METHOD

Make the sponge one day ahead.

TO MAKE THE ALMOND SPONGE

Preheat the oven to 347°F (175°C).

Line three 6-in (15-cm) sandwich pans with oil spray and wax paper.

In the bowl of an electric mixer, beat the egg yolks and vanilla. With the mixer on high speed, gradually add ⅓ cup (60 g) of the superfine sugar. Beat for about 5 minutes, until pale, thick, and light. Transfer the egg-yolk mixture to a large bowl and set aside.

Place the egg whites and salt in a bowl and, using the electric mixer, beat on medium speed until soft peaks form. Increase the speed to high and gradually add the remaining sugar. Beat for about 4 minutes, until stiff and glossy.

Fold the egg-white mixture into the egg-yolk mixture.

Fold the remaining dry ingredients into the egg mixture, a third at a time.

Transfer the batter to the lined pans and gently spread it toward the edges using a step palette knife. The batter should be higher around the edges of the pan than in the center, to ensure an even bake and cake height.

Bake for 25 to 30 minutes. The sponge is cooked when it springs back to the touch and the sides are coming away from the edges of the pan. To be absolutely sure, insert a knife into the middle of the sponge; if it is cooked, the knife will come out clean.

While baking, make the sugar syrup following the instructions on page 13 and let cool. Add vanilla extract to taste.

Once the sponges are baked, remove from the oven and let them rest for about 10 minutes.

Brush the tops of the sponges with vanilla syrup.

Once just warm, run a knife all the way around the sides of the pans, transfer the sponges to a wire rack, and let cool completely.

Once cool, wrap the sponges in plastic wrap and let them rest overnight at room temperature. This will ensure that all the moisture is sealed and the sponges are a good firm texture ready for trimming and layering.

TO MAKE THE COCONUT MERINGUE BUTTERCREAM

Make the meringue buttercream following the instructions on page 10.

Soften the creamed coconut following the instructions on the package and gently fold into the meringue buttercream.

TO ASSEMBLE THE CAKE

Trim the three sponge layers and sandwich them together using the coconut meringue buttercream.

Mask the top and sides of the cake with the remaining buttercream.

For full instructions on how to trim, layer, and mask your cake, turn to pages 150 to 153.

TO DECORATE

Place the dry unsweetened coconut in a medium bowl. Hold the chilled cake above the bowl at an angle and press the dry unsweetened coconut around the sides. Catch the excess coconut in the bowl.

If stored in the refrigerator, this cake will last for up to 5 days; however, it will taste at its best if consumed within 3 days of baking. Serve at room temperature.

SALTED CARAMEL CAKE

THIS CAKE ROCKS! SORRY TO BE SO BLUNT, BUT IT REALLY DOES. IT IS SMOOTH, GOOEY, STICKY, SWEET, AND SALTY, AND IS JAM-PACKED WITH LOTS OF CHOCOLATE AND CARAMEL. CAKE DOESN'T GET MUCH BETTER THAN THIS.

INGREDIENTS

For the caramel sponge
¼ cup (55 g) butter
½ cup plus 2 Tbsp (125 g) superfine sugar
¼ cup plus 2 Tbsp (75 g) packed dark brown sugar
2 tsp vanilla extract
2 eggs
Scant 1¼ cups (140 g) all-purpose flour
½ cup (120 ml) buttermilk
1½ tsp white wine vinegar
½ tsp baking soda

For the chocolate sponge
7 Tbsp (100 g) butter
1¾ cups (340 g) packed light brown sugar
½ cup (100 g) semisweet chocolate drops
(53% cocoa solids)
⅝ cup (150 ml) milk
3 medium eggs
Scant 2 cups (225 g) all-purpose flour
2¼ Tbsp unsweetened cocoa powder
¾ tsp baking soda
¾ tsp baking powder
A pinch of salt

For the vanilla sponge
7 Tbsp (100 g) butter
½ cup (100 g) superfine sugar
½ tsp vanilla extract
2 medium eggs
Generous ¾ cup (100 g) self-rising flour, sifted
A pinch of salt

For the vanilla syrup
⅞ cup (200 ml) water
1 cup (200 g) sugar
1 Tbsp vanilla extract

For the salted caramel
2¼ cups (450 g) sugar
⅝ cup (150 ml) water
Scant ¼ cup (45 g) glucose
1¼ cups (300 ml) whipping cream, slightly heated
½ cup (120 g) butter
½ tsp salt

For the chocolate ganache
3½ cups (600 g) semisweet Belgian chocolate
drops (53% cocoa solids)
Generous 1¾ cups (450 ml) whipping cream
Scant ¼ cup (60 g) glucose

EQUIPMENT

Baking tool kit (see page 8)
Layering tool kit (see page 8)
8-in (20-cm) round sandwich pan
Pastry bag
Toothpick

Makes one 8-in (20-cm) round cake, serving 12 to 16 generous slices.

METHOD

Make the sponges one day ahead.

TO MAKE THE CARAMEL SPONGE
Preheat the oven to 347°F (175°C).

Line one 8-in (20-cm) sandwich pan with oil spray and wax paper.

Place the butter, superfine sugar, dark brown sugar, and vanilla in an electric mixer and, using the paddle, beat at medium-high speed until pale and fluffy.

Lightly beat the eggs in a separate bowl or pitcher and, with the mixer on medium speed, slowly pour in the eggs. If the mixture starts to curdle, add 1 Tbsp of flour to bring it back together. Once combined, mix in the flour and buttermilk, beating at low speed until just incorporated.

In a small bowl, combine the vinegar and baking soda. Fold this quickly, but lightly, through the cake batter. Using a rubber spatula, fold through the batter to make sure everything is well combined.

Transfer the batter to the lined pan and gently spread it toward the edges with a step palette knife. Bake for 25 to 30 minutes. The sponge is cooked when it springs back to the touch and the sides are coming away from the edges of the pan. If you insert a clean knife into the center, it should come out clean. Remove from the oven and let rest for about 10 minutes.

While the sponge is baking, make the vanilla syrup following the instructions on page 13 and using the amounts given on page 34. Once the sponge is baked, remove from the oven and let rest for about 10 minutes. Brush the top of the sponge with the vanilla syrup. When just warm, run a knife all the way around the sides of the pan, transfer the sponge to a wire rack, and let cool completely.

Wrap the cooled sponge in plastic wrap and let it rest overnight at room temperature. This will ensure that all the moisture is sealed and the sponge is the perfect firm texture for trimming and layering.

TO MAKE THE CHOCOLATE SPONGE
Preheat the oven to 325°F (160°C).

Line one 8-in (20-cm) sandwich pan with oil spray and wax paper.

Put the butter and half of the brown sugar in an electric mixer and, using the paddle, beat at medium-high speed until pale and fluffy.

Meanwhile, place the chocolate drops, milk, and remaining sugar in a deep saucepan and bring to a boil, stirring occasionally.

Slowly add the eggs to the mixer. Sift together the flour, cocoa, baking soda, baking powder, and salt and add to the mixture while beating on slow speed.

Pour the hot chocolate mixture into a pitcher and slowly add it to the batter while mixing on slow speed. Take care, as the hot mixture could splash you. Once combined, pour the hot batter into the prepared pan.

Bake for 20 to 30 minutes. If you insert a clean knife into the middle of the sponge to check that it is cooked, the knife will come out almost clean—this chocolate cake should be slightly gooey in texture.

Once cooked, let the cake rest in the pan for about 10 minutes, then transfer to a wire rack to cool. Once completely cool, wrap the sponge in plastic wrap and let rest overnight at room temperature.

TO MAKE THE VANILLA SPONGE
Preheat the oven to 347°F (175°C).

Line one 8-in (20-cm) sandwich pan with oil spray and wax paper. Place the butter, superfine sugar, and vanilla in an electric mixer and, using the paddle, beat at medium-high speed until pale and fluffy.

Lightly beat the eggs in a separate bowl or pitcher and slowly pour into the mixture with the mixer on medium speed. If the mixture starts to curdle, add 1 Tbsp of flour to bring it back together.

Once the mixture is well incorporated, mix in the flour and salt at low speed until just combined. Using a rubber spatula, fold through the batter to make sure everything is well combined.

Transfer the batter to the lined pan and spread toward the edges with a step palette knife. The batter should be high around the edges and dip down in the middle, to ensure an even bake and level height.

Bake for 20 to 25 minutes. Check that the sponge is cooked (as with the caramel sponge, a knife pushed into the center should come out clean).

Once the sponge is baked, remove from the oven and let rest for about 10 minutes. Brush the top of the sponge with the vanilla syrup.

When the sponge is just warm, run a knife all the way around the sides of the pan, transfer to a wire rack, and let cool completely.

Wrap the cooled sponge in plastic wrap and let rest overnight at room temperature.

TO MAKE THE SALTED CARAMEL
Heat the sugar, water, and glucose in a medium saucepan over moderate heat, stirring continuously with a rubber spatula. The sugar will melt into a thick amber liquid as you stir. Do not let the sugar burn.

Once the sugar has caramelized, slowly add the cream. Be careful here, as the caramel will bubble rapidly when the cream is added.

Add the butter to the caramel, stirring until melted. This will take 2 to 3 minutes. Let the mixture boil for 1 minute—it will rise in the pan as it boils.

Remove the caramel from the heat and stir in ½ tsp of salt. Cover well and cool before using.

TO MAKE THE CHOCOLATE GANACHE
Make the ganache following the instructions on page 13, using the amounts given on page 34, and let cool to room temperature.

TO ASSEMBLE THE CAKE
Trim the three sponge layers.

Fill a pastry bag with chocolate ganache, take the chocolate and caramel sponges, and pipe a ring of ganache around the edge of each one.

Using a palette knife, fill each ring with salted caramel, then sandwich the layers together with the chocolate at the bottom, caramel in the middle, and vanilla on the top. See pages 150 to 151 for full instructions on how to trim and layer your cakes.

Place the cake on a turntable and mask with chocolate ganache (pages 152 to 153). Chill for at least 2 hours.

TO DECORATE
Place a wire rack over a large plate or tray. Pour the remaining ganache into a microwavable pitcher. Heat the ganache in the microwave until smooth.

Place the cake on the wire rack and pour the ganache over the cake, ensuring that the sides are well covered (steps 1 to 3).

Use a large palette knife to smooth the top and remove any excess ganache (step 4).

Put the remaining salted caramel into a pastry bag and pipe a spiral pattern on top of the cake. If the caramel is too stiff, soften in the microwave (steps 5 to 7).

Using a toothpick, make lines from the center of the spiral to the edges of the cake to create a spiderweb pattern (steps 8 to 9).

Using a large palette knife, carefully lift the cake from the rack and place it on your cake stand.

To maintain the sheen on the ganache, let the glaze set at room temperature.

The ganache that dripped onto the plate can be reused. Any remaining ganache can be kept for up to 2 weeks in an airtight container in the refrigerator.

Store the cake in the refrigerator if not serving on the same day. Always serve at room temperature. The cake tastes best within the first 3 days of baking, but will last for up to one week if stored in the refrigerator.

SALTED CARAMEL CAKE

VANILLA CLOUD CAKE

AS THE NAME SUGGESTS, THIS CAKE HAS A HEAVENLY LIGHT TEXTURE AND
TASTES SMOOTH AND SQUISHY. IT IS THE PERFECT CAKE FOR KIDS'
BIRTHDAYS AND BABY CELEBRATIONS.

INGREDIENTS

For the chiffon sponge

3 oz (80 g) egg yolks

1 Tbsp vanilla extract

1⅛ cups (225 g) superfine sugar

5 Tbsp (75 ml) vegetable oil

5¾ oz (165 g) egg whites

A pinch of cream of tartar

A pinch of salt

Scant 1 cup (225 g) all-purpose flour

1 Tbsp baking powder

½ cup (120 ml) milk

**For the vanilla
meringue buttercream**

1⅓ cups (270 g) superfine sugar

¼ cup (67 ml) water

4¾ oz (135 g) egg whites

1½ cups (330 g) butter

1 Tbsp vanilla extract

A little pink food paste color

For the vanilla syrup

⅝ cup (150 ml) water

¾ cup (150 g) superfine sugar

1 Tbsp vanilla extract

For the decoration

Powdered sugar, for dusting

EQUIPMENT

Baking tool kit (see page 8)

Layering tool kit (see page 8)

Three 6-in (15-cm) round sandwich pans

Bows & Swags or cloud stencil

(both available from Peggy's sugarcraft collection)

Makes one 6-in (15-cm) pink cake, serving 8 generous slices.
Multiply the amounts by 3 for a 10-in (25-cm) cake.

METHOD

Make the sponge one day ahead.

TO MAKE THE CHIFFON SPONGE
Preheat the oven to 347°F (175°C).

Line three 6-in (15-cm) sandwich pans with oil spray and wax paper.

Place the egg yolks, vanilla extract, and a little of the sugar in an electric mixer and using the whisk attachment, beat until pale and fluffy. Add the oil slowly and continue to beat until thick and pale.

Beat the egg whites, cream of tartar, and salt in the mixer and, using the whisk attachment, beat at medium-high speed until the mixture forms soft peaks.

With the mixer still running, slowly pour in the remaining sugar and beat until the mixture is glossy and holds stiff peaks.

Sift the flour and baking powder into a medium bowl and add to the egg-yolk mixture a little at a time, gently folding after each addition to incorporate. Add the milk and fold in the stiff egg whites.

Transfer the batter to the lined pans and gently spread it toward the edges with a step palette knife. The batter should be higher around the edges of each pan and dipping in the center; this will ensure that the sponges bake evenly and are level.

Bake for 20 to 25 minutes. Insert a clean knife into the middle of each sponge; if they are cooked, the knife will come out clean.

While baking, make the sugar syrup following the instructions on page 13. Add the vanilla extract and mix well.

Once the sponges are baked, remove from the oven and let rest for about 10 minutes. Brush the tops of the sponges with vanilla syrup (setting aside some for the assembling stage and storing it in the refrigerator overnight).

Once just warm, run a knife all the way around the sides of the pans, remove the sponges, and let cool completely on a wire rack.

Once cool, wrap the sponges in plastic wrap and let rest overnight at room temperature. This will ensure that all the moisture is sealed and that the sponges are a good firm texture for trimming and layering.

TO MAKE THE VANILLA MERINGUE BUTTERCREAM
Follow the instructions for meringue buttercream on page 10.

Mix a small amount of the buttercream with the vanilla extract and a little pink food color until all the color has dissolved.

Slowly add the mixture to the remaining buttercream and fold through gently, taking care not to overwork.

TO ASSEMBLE THE CAKE
Trim the three sponge layers, soak with more of the vanilla syrup, and sandwich together using the pink vanilla meringue buttercream. For full instructions, see pages 150 to 151.

Place the cake on a turntable and mask the top and sides with the remaining meringue buttercream. For a detailed guide to masking, turn to pages 152 to 153.

TO DECORATE
Center the cake stencil on the top of the cold masked cake and dust the surface liberally with powdered sugar. Carefully lift the stencil off the cake to reveal the ribbon pattern.

Store the cake in the refrigerator if not serving immediately, and serve at room temperature. Keep away from heat or direct sunlight. The cake tastes best if consumed within 3 days of baking, but can last for up to a week if stored in the refrigerator.

TO MAKE THE LIGHT BLUE CLOUD CAKE
Triple the sponge recipe and bake in three 10-in (25-cm) sandwich pans.

Slice each layer in half and sandwich with light blue vanilla meringue buttercream.

Mask with light blue vanilla meringue buttercream, and use a cloud stencil to decorate.

COOKIES AND CREAM CAKE

FOLLOWING THE SUCCESS OF MY CUPCAKE VERSION OF THIS CAKE—WHICH WAS
DESCRIBED BY ONE OF MY CUSTOMERS AS "LIFE CHANGING"—I FELT COMPELLED
TO TURN IT INTO A LAYER CAKE. SEE WHAT YOU THINK …

INGREDIENTS

For the cookies & cream sponge
1 ¼ cups (300 g) butter
1 ½ cups (300 g) superfine sugar
1 Tbsp vanilla extract
6 eggs
2 ½ cups (300 g) self-rising flour
¾ tsp baking powder
A pinch of salt
5 ¼ oz (150 g) Oreo cookies, crushed

For the vanilla syrup
⅝ cup (150 ml) water
¾ cup (150 g) sugar
1 tsp vanilla extract

For the cookie frosting
1 cup (250 g) cream cheese, softened
Generous 1 cup (250 g) unsalted butter, softened
5 ¼ cups (625 g) powdered sugar, sifted
1 Tbsp vanilla extract
7 oz (200 g) Oreo cookies, finely crushed

For the decoration
16 mini Oreo cookies

EQUIPMENT

Baking tool kit (see page 8)
Layering tool kit (see page 8)
Four 6-in (15-cm) round sandwich pans
Pastry bag
Medium round piping tip

Makes one 6-in (15-cm) round cake, serving 8 generous slices.

METHOD
Make the sponge one day ahead.

TO MAKE THE COOKIE AND CREAM SPONGE
Preheat the oven to 344°F (170°C).

Line four 6-in (15-cm) sandwich pans with oil spray and wax paper.

Place the butter, sugar, and vanilla extract in an electric mixer and, using the paddle, beat at medium-high speed until pale and fluffy.

Lightly beat the eggs in a separate bowl or pitcher and, with the mixer set at medium speed, slowly pour into the butter mixture. If it starts to curdle, add 1 Tbsp of flour to bring it back together.

Sift in the flour, baking powder, and salt and fold until the batter is just combined.

Add the crushed cookies.

Bake for 20 to 25 minutes. The sponges are cooked when they spring back to the touch and the sides are coming away from the edges of the pans. To double-check, you could insert a clean knife into the middle of the sponges; if they are cooked, the knife will come out clean.

While the sponges are in the oven, make the vanilla sugar syrup following the instructions on page 13. Add the vanilla extract to taste.

Once the sponges are baked, remove from the oven and let them rest for about 10 minutes.

Brush the tops of the sponges with vanilla syrup (setting aside some for the assembling stage and storing it in the refrigerator overnight).

Once just warm, run a knife all the way around the sides of the pans, remove the sponges, and let cool completely on a wire rack.

Wrap the cooled sponges in plastic wrap and let them rest overnight at room temperature. This will ensure that all the moisture is sealed and the sponges are the perfect firm texture for trimming and layering.

TO MAKE THE COOKIE FROSTING
Make a cream-cheese frosting following the instructions on page 12.

Gently fold in the vanilla and crushed Oreo cookies and chill for at least 2 hours or until set.

TO ASSEMBLE THE CAKE
Trim the four sponge layers, soak with more vanilla syrup, and sandwich together using the cookie frosting. See pages 150 to 151 for more instructions on how to trim and layer the sponges.

Mask the top and sides of the cake with the remaining cookies and frosting. See pages 152 to 153 for a step-by-step guide to masking.

TO DECORATE
Place the remaining cookie frosting in a pastry bag fitted with a medium round tip.

Pipe 16 evenly spaced small dots around the edge of the cake and top each one with a mini Oreo cookie.

If stored in the refrigerator, this cake will last for up to 5 days; however, it tastes best if consumed within the first 3 days of baking. Serve at room temperature.

LEMON, RASPBERRY, AND ROSE CAKE

THIS IS A LOVELY FLAVOR COMBINATION THAT WORKS REALLY WELL FOR A SUMMER OCCASION SUCH AS A GARDEN TEA PARTY. FOR A CONTEMPORARY LOOK, I HAVE COLOR-BLOCKED THE TOP OF THE CAKE WITH A LAYER OF ROSE PETAL FRAGMENTS. IF YOU PREFER A MORE TRADITIONAL DESIGN, YOU COULD RECREATE THE CAKE SHOWN ON THE COVER INSTEAD.

INGREDIENTS

For the lemon sponge
⅞ cup (200 g) salted butter
I cup (200 g) superfine sugar
Zest of 2 unwaxed lemons
4 medium eggs, at room temperature
1⅔ cups (200 g) self-rising flour, sifted

For the lemon syrup
⅝ cup (150 ml) lemon juice
¾ cup (150 g) superfine sugar

For the raspberry meringue buttercream
1⅓ cups (270 g) superfine sugar
¼ cup (67 ml) water
4¾ oz (135 g) egg whites
1½ cups (330 g) butter
5¾ oz (160 g) raspberry puree
Raspberry extract (to taste)

For the decoration
About 3 Tbsp rose petal fragments, glazed
Powdered sugar and fresh raspberries
(for cover design only)

EQUIPMENT

Baking tool kit (see page 8)
Layering tool kit (see page 8)
Three 6-in (15-cm) round sandwich pans
For cover design only:
Peggy's cake stencil (included with this book)
Pastry bag
Medium star piping tip

Makes one 6-in (15-cm) cake, serving **8** generous slices.

METHOD

Make the sponge one day ahead.

TO MAKE THE LEMON SPONGE
Preheat the oven to 347°F (175°C).

Line three 6-in (15-cm) sandwich pans with oil spray and wax paper.

Place the butter, superfine sugar, and lemon zest in an electric mixer and, using the paddle, beat at medium-high speed until pale and fluffy.

Lightly beat the eggs in a separate bowl or pitcher and, with the mixer set at medium speed, slowly pour into the mixture. If it starts to curdle, add 1 Tbsp of flour to bring it back together.

Once the butter, sugar, and eggs are combined, add the flour with the mixer set at low speed, until just incorporated.

Using the rubber spatula, fold through the batter to make sure everything is well combined.

Transfer the batter to the lined pans and gently spread toward the edges with a step palette knife. The batter should be higher around the edges of the pans than in the center, to ensure an even bake and level cake height.

Bake for 20 to 25 minutes. The sponges are cooked when they spring back to the touch and the sides are coming away from the edges of the pan. You could also insert a clean knife into the middle of each sponge; if they are cooked, the knife will come out clean.

While the sponges are in the oven, make a lemon sugar syrup following the instructions on page 13, but replacing the water with lemon juice.

Once the sponges are baked, remove from the oven and let them rest for about 10 minutes. Brush the tops of the sponges with lemon syrup (setting aside some for the assembling stage and storing it in the refrigerator overnight).

Once just warm, run a knife all the way around the sides of the pans, remove the sponges, and let cool completely on a wire rack.

Wrap the cooled sponges in plastic wrap and let rest overnight at room temperature. This will ensure that all the moisture is sealed and the sponges firm up to the ideal texture for trimming and layering.

TO MAKE THE RASPBERRY MERINGUE BUTTERCREAM
Put the raspberry puree in a small saucepan, bring to a boil, and simmer until reduced to half. Chill until cool.

Make the meringue buttercream following the instructions on page 10.

Add a little meringue buttercream to the raspberry puree and mix until well combined.

Gently fold into the remaining meringue buttercream and add the raspberry extract to taste. If the mixture splits, whip it with an electric mixer until smooth.

TO ASSEMBLE THE CAKE
Trim the three sponge layers, soak with more lemon syrup, and sandwich together using some of the raspberry meringue buttercream. If you wish to recreate the cake shown on the front of the book, sprinkle the rose petal fragments between the layers. For full instructions on how to trim and layer your cake, turn to pages 150 to 151.

Use meringue buttercream to mask the top and sides of the cake (pages 152 to 153).

TO DECORATE
Generously sprinkle the rose petal fragments over the top of the cake.

If you are recreating the design shown on the cover, decorate the top of the cake using the stencil and a good dusting of powdered sugar, then pipe small rosettes of raspberry meringue buttercream around the edge and finish with fresh raspberries.

FRENCH VIOLET CAKE
(GÂTEAU AUX FLEUR DE VIOLETTES)

THIS RECIPE PAYS TRIBUTE TO A BEAUTIFUL FRENCH ARTISAN VILLAGE CALLED "TOURRETTES-SUR-LOUP," WHERE I STAYED LAST SUMMER. IT IS RENOWNED FOR ITS CULTURE OF VIOLETS AND CONFECTIONS, WHICH INSPIRED ME TO CREATE THIS DELECTABLE ELEGANT CAKE.

INGREDIENTS

For the chiffon sponge
3 oz (80 g) egg yolks
1⅛ cups (225 g) superfine sugar
5 Tbsp (75 ml) vegetable oil
5¾ oz (165 g) egg whites
A pinch of cream of tartar
A pinch of salt
2 tsp vanilla extract
Generous 1¾ cups (225 g) all-purpose flour
1 Tbsp baking powder
½ cup (120 ml) milk

For the vanilla syrup
⅝ cup (150 ml) water
¾ cup (150 g) superfine sugar
1 Tbsp vanilla extract

For the violet meringue buttercream
1⅓ cups (270 g) superfine sugar
¼ cup (67 ml) water
4¾ oz (135 g) egg whites
1½ cups (330 g) butter
1 handful of violet petal fragments
A few drops of violet extract (to taste)
A little violet food paste color

For the decoration
Powdered sugar
1 Tbsp candied whole violets

EQUIPMENT

Baking tool kit (see page 8)
Layering tool kit (see page 8)
Three 6-in (15-cm) round sandwich pans
Peggy's cake stencil (included with this book)
Pastry bag
Medium star piping tip

Makes one 6-in (15-cm) cake, serving 8 generous slices.

METHOD

Make the sponge one day ahead.

TO MAKE THE CHIFFON SPONGE
Preheat the oven to 347°F (175°C).

Line three 6-in (15-cm) sandwich pans with oil spray and wax paper.

Place the egg yolks in an electric mixer with a little of the sugar and, using the whisk attachment, beat at medium-high speed until pale and fluffy. Add the oil slowly and beat until thick and pale.

Put the egg whites, cream of tartar, and salt in the electric mixer and, again using the whisk attachment, beat at medium-high speed until the mixture forms soft peaks.

With the mixer still running, slowly pour in the remaining sugar and beat until the mixture is glossy and holds stiff peaks. Beat in the vanilla extract.

Sift the flour and baking powder into a medium bowl and gradually add to the egg-yolk mixture, gently folding after each addition to incorporate. Add the milk and fold in the stiff egg whites.

Transfer the batter to the lined pans and gently spread it toward the edges with a step palette knife.

Bake for 20 to 25 minutes. The sponge is cooked when it springs back to the touch and the sides are coming away from the edges of the pan. To double-check, you could insert a clean knife into the middle of the sponge; if it is cooked, the knife will come out clean.

While the sponges are in the oven, make the sugar syrup following the instructions on page 13, then add the vanilla extract and mix well.

Once the sponges are baked, remove from the oven and let them rest for about 10 minutes. Brush the tops of the sponges with vanilla syrup (setting aside some for the assembling stage and storing it in the refrigerator overnight).

Run a knife all the way around the sides of the pans and transfer the sponges to a wire rack and let cool completely.

Once cool, wrap the sponges in plastic wrap and let rest overnight at room temperature. This will ensure that all the moisture is sealed and the sponges are a nice firm texture, ready for trimming and layering.

TO MAKE THE VIOLET MERINGUE BUTTERCREAM
Make some meringue buttercream following the instructions on page 10.

Take 7 oz (200 g) of the meringue buttercream and fold through the violet petal fragments and violet extract (add to taste). This will be used for the filling.

To the remaining buttercream add a little violet food paste color and violet extract (add to taste). This will be used for masking.

TO ASSEMBLE THE CAKE
Trim the three sponge layers, soak the tops with vanilla syrup, and sandwich together using the violet meringue buttercream with the petal fragments added. Turn to pages 150 to 151 for instructions on how to trim and layer your cake.

Place the cake on a turntable and mask with the violet-colored meringue buttercream. See pages 152 to 153 for advice on how to mask the cake.

Chill the cake for at least 1 hour, or until the buttercream is set, before applying the final coat.

TO DECORATE THE CAKE
Center the stencil on top of the chilled cake (step 1, overleaf) and dust liberally with powdered sugar, ensuring that all the cutouts are well coated (step 2). Carefully lift the stencil off the cake.

Attach the star tip to the pastry bag and fill with the remaining violet-colored meringue buttercream. Pipe rosettes around the edge of the cake, spacing them evenly over the pattern (steps 3 to 4).

Top each rosette with a candied violet.

Refrigerate if not serving immediately, and serve at room temperature. Keep away from heat and direct sunlight. This cake is best eaten within 3 days, but will last for up to 1 week if stored in the refrigerator.

RED VELVET CAKE

THIS IS AN ALL-TIME CLASSIC AND A FIRM FAVORITE AT MY CAKE SHOP—PERFECT
IF YOU WANT TO BAKE YOUR WAY INTO SOMEONE'S HEART.

INGREDIENTS

For the red velvet sponge

½ cup (105 g) butter

1⅓ cups (275 g) superfine sugar

1 tsp vanilla extract

About ½ tsp extra-red food color

1 cup (250 ml) buttermilk

2 medium eggs

Scant 2 cups (235 g) all-purpose flour

1 Tbsp unsweetened cocoa powder

2 pinches of salt

1 tsp baking soda

1¼ tsp white wine vinegar

For the vanilla frosting

1 cup (250 g) whole cream cheese, softened slightly

Generous 1 cup (250 g) unsalted butter, softened

5¼ cups (625 g) powdered sugar, sifted

1 Tbsp vanilla extract

For the decoration

Red velvet cake crumbs

EQUIPMENT

Baking tool kit (see page 8)

Layering tool kit (see page 8)

Three 6-in (15-cm) shallow round sandwich pans

Heart cake stencil (you can easily make your
own using a sheet of card or paper and a pair
of scissors)

Makes one 6-in (15-cm) cake, serving 8 generous slices.

METHOD

Make the sponge one day ahead.

TO MAKE THE RED VELVET SPONGE
Preheat the oven to 344°F (170°C).

Line three 6-in (15-cm) sandwich pans with oil spray and wax paper.

Place the butter, superfine sugar, and vanilla in an electric mixer and, using the paddle, beat at medium-high speed until pale and fluffy.

Mix the red food color with the buttermilk, making sure there are no lumps.

Lightly beat the eggs in a separate bowl or pitcher and, with the mixer set at medium speed, slowly pour into the butter mixture. If the mixture starts to curdle, add 1 Tbsp of flour to bring it back together.

Sift the flour, cocoa powder, and salt together and, once the butter, sugar, and eggs are combined, add to the mixer with the colored buttermilk, and beat at low speed until just incorporated.

Whisk together the baking soda and vinegar and quickly add to the cake batter.

Using the rubber spatula, fold through the batter to make sure everything is well combined.

Transfer the batter to the lined pans and gently spread it toward the edges with a step palette knife.

Bake for 20 to 25 minutes. The sponge is cooked when it springs back to the touch and the sides are coming away from the edges of the pan. You could also insert a clean knife into the middle of the sponge; if it is cooked, the knife will come out clean.

Once the sponges are baked, remove from the oven and let rest for about 10 minutes.

When the sponges are just warm, run a knife all the way around the sides of the pans, transfer to a wire rack, and let cool completely.

Once cool, wrap the sponges in plastic wrap and let them rest overnight at room temperature.

This will ensure that all the moisture is sealed and the sponges firm up to the ideal texture for trimming and layering.

TO MAKE THE VANILLA FROSTING
Make a cream-cheese frosting following the instructions on page 12, then flavor with the vanilla extract.

Chill for at least 2 hours, or until set.

TO ASSEMBLE THE CAKE
Trim the sponges (setting aside the trimmings for decoration) and sandwich the layers together using the vanilla frosting. See pages 150 to 151 for trimming and layering tips.

Mask the top and sides of the cake using the remaining vanilla frosting. See pages 152 to 153 for instructions on how to mask the cake.

TO DECORATE
Preheat the oven to 212°F (100°C).

Take all the trimmings from the sponges and place them on a lined rimmed baking sheet.

Put them in the oven to dry out, until hard.

Put the cake trimmings in a food processor and whiz until you have a fine crumb.

Center the heart cake stencil on the top of the cake, and dust the surface liberally with the red velvet cake crumbs.

Carefully lift the stencil off the cake to reveal the heart pattern.

Store the cake in the refrigerator if not serving immediately. The cake has a shelf life of up to 5 days but tastes best if consumed within 3 days.

Serve at room temperature.

TOFFEE APPLE CAKE

THIS IS A DELICIOUSLY MOIST APPLE CAKE, PACKED WITH NUTS AND SPICES.
I DECORATED IT WITH TINY APPLES FROM MY NEIGHBOR'S GARDEN,
DIPPED IN GOLDEN CARAMEL.

INGREDIENTS

For the spiced apple sponge
1 cup (225 g) unsalted butter
1⅛ cups (225 g) packed light brown sugar
1 Tbsp vanilla extract
4 medium eggs
2 cups (240 g) self-rising flour
1 Tbsp ground cinnamon
A pinch of salt
7 oz (200 g) cooking apples, peeled and chopped
⅓ cup (50 g) hazelnuts, toasted and finely chopped
Zest of 1 unwaxed lemon

For the vanilla syrup
⅝ cup (150 ml) water
¾ cup (150 g) superfine sugar
1 Tbsp vanilla extract (or to taste)

For the caramel frosting
1 cup (250 g) cream cheese, softened
Generous 1 cup (250 g) unsalted butter, softened
5¼ cups (625 g) powdered sugar, sifted
5¼ oz (150 g) dulce de leche (alternatively, use caramel made from sweetened condensed milk)

For the dipping caramel
1⅛ cups (225 g) packed brown sugar
½ cup (110 ml) water
½ tsp vinegar
1 Tbsp (30 ml) light corn syrup
2 Tbsp (25 g) butter

For the decoration
3 mini crab apples
Bay leaves or apple leaves

EQUIPMENT

Baking tool kit (see page 8)
Layering tool kit (see page 8)
Three 6-in (15-cm) round sandwich pans
Sugar thermometer
Pastry bag
Large round piping tip

Makes one 6-in (15-cm) round cake, serving 8 generous slices.

METHOD

Make the sponge one day ahead.

TO MAKE THE SPICED APPLE SPONGE
Preheat the oven to 347°F (175°C).

Line three 6-in (15-cm) sandwich pans with oil spray and wax paper.

Place the butter, sugar, and vanilla extract in an electric mixer and, using the paddle, beat at medium-high speed until pale and fluffy.

Lightly beat the eggs in a separate bowl or pitcher and slowly pour into the mixer, while beating at medium speed. If the mixture starts to curdle, add 1 Tbsp of flour to bring it back together.

Sift the flour, cinnamon, and salt into a bowl and fold into the batter until just combined.

Fold in the apple, hazelnuts, and lemon zest, transfer the batter to the lined pans, and gently spread it out toward the edges with a step palette knife. The batter should be higher around the edges than in the middle, to ensure that the cake bakes evenly and that the height is level.

Bake for 20 to 25 minutes. The sponges are cooked when they spring back to the touch and the sides are starting to come away from the edges of the pans. To double-check, you could insert a clean knife into the middle of the sponge; if it is cooked, the knife will come out clean.

While the sponges are in the oven, make the sugar syrup following the instructions on page 13, then add the vanilla extract to taste.

When the sponges are baked, remove from the oven and let them rest for about 10 minutes. Brush the tops of the sponges with vanilla syrup (setting aside some for the assembling stage and storing it in the refrigerator overnight).

Once just warm, run a knife all the way around the sides of the pans, remove the sponges, and let cool completely on a wire rack.

When the sponges are cool, wrap them in plastic wrap and let them rest overnight at room temperature. This will ensure that all the moisture is sealed and that the sponges are a good firm texture for trimming and layering.

TO MAKE THE CARAMEL FROSTING
Make a cream-cheese frosting following the instructions on page 12, then gently fold in the dulce de leche.

TO MAKE THE DIPPING CARAMEL
Put the sugar and water in a saucepan and place over moderate heat, stirring lightly with a rubber spatula, until the sugar has dissolved.

Stir in the vinegar, syrup, and butter, then bring to a boil, stirring continuously until the caramel reaches 280°F (138°C).

Immediately dip the apples in the caramel and let harden on a lightly oiled tray or wax paper. (Steps 1 to 4, opposite.)

Dip the tips of the bay leaf stalks in the caramel and stick them to the tops of the apples.

TO ASSEMBLE THE CAKE
Trim the three sponge layers and soak the tops with vanilla syrup, as shown on pages 150 to 151.

Put the frosting in a pastry bag fitted with a large round tip. Pipe a ring of large dots around the outside of the bottom layer, then pipe a swirl in the center and place the second sponge layer on top. Repeat the piping on the next layer, then put the last sponge in place. (Steps 5 to 6.)

TO DECORATE
Repeat the piped pattern on the top of the cake and, using a palette knife, drag each dot toward the middle. (Steps 7 to 9.)

Place 3 mini toffee apples in the center.

This cake has a shelf life of up to 3 days if stored in the refrigerator. Serve at room temperature.

BLACK AND WHITE DEVIL'S FOOD CAKE

THIS CHOCOLATE AND VANILLA CAKE IS TRULY DELICIOUS AND THE MONOCHROME LAYERS LOOK STRIKING WHEN CUT INTO SLICES.

INGREDIENTS

For the devil's food sponge

1½ cups (150 g) unsweetened cocoa powder, sifted
1½ cups (300 g) packed dark brown sugar
3 cups (750 ml) boiling water
1¾ cups (375 g) unsalted butter
2¼ cups (450 g) packed light brown sugar
2 Tbsp vanilla extract
6 extra-large eggs
Scant 5⅔ cups (675 g) all-purpose flour, sifted
1½ tsp baking powder, sifted
1½ tsp baking soda, sifted
A pinch of salt
A little black food color

For the sugar syrup

⅞ cup (200 ml) water
1 cup (200 g) sugar

For the vanilla frosting

1½ cups (375 g) cream cheese, softened
1¾ cups (375 g) unsalted butter, softened
Scant 8 cups (950 g) powdered sugar, sifted
1 Tbsp vanilla extract

For the decoration

Devil's food cake crumbs

EQUIPMENT

Baking tool kit (see page 8)
Layering tool kit (see page 8)
Five 8-in (20-cm) round sandwich pans
Patterned side scraper

Makes one 6-in (15-cm) round cake, serving 8 to 12 slices.

METHOD

Make the sponge one day ahead.

TO MAKE THE DEVIL'S FOOD SPONGE

Preheat the oven to 347°F (175°C).

Line five 8-in (20-cm) sandwich pans with oil spray and wax paper. (The sponges can be sliced in half if you don't have enough pans.)

Put the cocoa and dark sugar in a bowl and pour over the boiling water. Whisk to combine, then set aside.

In an electric mixer, cream together the butter, light brown sugar, and vanilla extract, beating well until pale and fluffy.

Lightly beat the eggs in a separate bowl or pitcher and slowly pour into the mixer, set at medium speed.

Combine the dry ingredients, then gradually add to the mixer, alternating with the cocoa mixture. Scrape the sides of the bowl with a spatula, to ensure that everything is incorporated.

Fold in the black food color until the batter takes on a muddy brown color, then transfer to the lined pans.

Bake for 20 to 25 minutes. The sponge is cooked when it springs back to the touch and the sides are coming away from the edges of the pan. You could also insert a clean knife into the middle of the sponge; if it is cooked, the knife will come out clean.

While baking, make the sugar syrup following the instructions on page 13 but using the amounts given on page 68.

Once the sponges are baked, remove from the oven and let them rest for about 10 minutes.

Brush the tops of the sponges with sugar syrup (setting aside some for the assembling stage and storing it in the refrigerator overnight).

Once just warm, run a knife all the way around the sides of the pans, remove the sponges, and let cool completely on a wire rack.

Wrap the cooled sponges in plastic wrap and let them rest overnight at room temperature. This will ensure that all the moisture is sealed and that the sponges are the perfect firm texture for trimming and layering.

TO MAKE THE VANILLA FROSTING

Make a cream-cheese frosting following the instructions on page 12, using the amounts given on page 68.

Gently fold in the vanilla extract and chill for at least 2 hours, or until set.

TO ASSEMBLE THE CAKE

Trim the five sponge layers, soak the tops with sugar syrup, and sandwich together using the vanilla frosting. Set aside the trimmings for the decoration. See pages 150 to 151 for trimming and layering instructions.

Mask the top and sides of the cake with the remaining vanilla cream-cheese frosting (pages 152 to 153).

To apply the final coat of masking, use a side scraper with a patterned edge.

TO DECORATE

Preheat the oven to 212°F (100°C).

Place all the cake trimmings on a lined rimmed baking sheet and put them in the oven to dry out.

Once dry and hard, put the trimmings into a food processor and whiz until you have a fine dust.

Sprinkle the chocolate dust evenly over the top of the cake.

PASSION FRUIT AND MASCARPONE CAKE

A REFRESHING TROPICAL CAKE FOR HOT SUMMER DAYS.

For the vanilla sponge
⅞ cup (200 g) butter
1 cup (200 g) superfine sugar
1 Tbsp vanilla extract
4 eggs
1⅔ cups (200 g) self-rising flour, sifted

For the vanilla syrup
⅝ cup (150 ml) water
¾ cup (150 g) sugar
1 tsp vanilla extract (or to taste)

For the mango frosting
⅞ cup (200 g) unsalted butter, softened
Scant 4¼ cups (500 g) powdered sugar
1¼ cups (300 g) mascarpone, softened slightly
1 oz (30 g) mango puree

For the passion fruit jelly
3 large gelatin leaves
7 oz (200 g) passion fruit puree
Scant ¼ cup (50 ml) water
¼ cup (50 g) sugar
2 passion fruit

To decorate
7 oz (200 g) coconut shavings

Baking tool kit (see page 8)
Layering tool kit (see page 8)
Three 6-in (15-cm) round sandwich pans
Baking sheet
Blowtorch (if needed)

Makes one 6-in (15-cm) cake, serving 8 generous slices.

METHOD
Make the sponge one day ahead.

TO MAKE THE VANILLA SPONGE
Preheat the oven to 347°F (175°C).

Line three 6-in (15-cm) sandwich pans with oil spray and wax paper.

Place the butter, superfine sugar, and vanilla in an electric mixer and, using the paddle, beat at medium-high speed until pale and fluffy.

Lightly beat the eggs in a separate bowl or pitcher and slowly pour into the mixer, beating at medium speed. If the mixture starts to curdle, add a little flour.

Once the butter, sugar, and eggs are combined, mix the flour at low speed until it is just incorporated. Using a rubber spatula, fold through the batter to make sure everything is well combined.

Bake for 20 to 25 minutes. When the sponge springs back to the touch and the sides are coming away from the edges of the pan, it is cooked. You could also insert a clean knife into the center of the sponge; if it is cooked, the knife will come out clean.

While the sponges are baking, make the vanilla sugar syrup by following the instructions on page 13, then adding vanilla extract to taste.

Once the sponges are baked, remove from the oven and let them rest for about 10 minutes. Using a pastry brush, soak the tops of the sponges with some of the vanilla syrup.

When just warm, run a knife all the way around the sides of the pans, transfer the sponges to a wire rack, and let cool completely.

Wrap the cooled sponges in plastic wrap and let rest overnight at room temperature. This will seal in all the moisture and firm up the sponges so they are the perfect texture for trimming and layering.

TO MAKE THE MANGO FROSTING
Make some mascarpone frosting following the instructions on page 12.

Gently fold in the mango puree. Chill for about 2 hours, or until set.

TO MAKE THE PASSION FRUIT JELLY
Soak the leaf gelatin in cold water for about 3 minutes.

Put the passion fruit puree, water, and sugar in a small saucepan and bring to a boil. Remove from the heat and add the drained leaf gelatin. Stir well and pass through a strainer. Add the pulp of the fresh passion fruit.

Line two 6-in (15-cm) round cake pans with plastic wrap. Divide the jelly mixture between the two pans and refrigerate for 30 minutes to 1 hour, or until set.

TO TOAST THE COCONUT SHAVINGS
Preheat the oven to 347°F (175°C).

Spread out the coconut shavings on a baking sheet and put in the oven for about 5 to 10 minutes, making sure all sides are toasted.

TO ASSEMBLE THE CAKE
Trim the three sponges and soak the tops with vanilla syrup, according to the instructions given on pages 150 to 151.

Spread a layer of mango frosting over the first sponge, then place the second sponge on top. Spread the second sponge with a thin layer of frosting, followed by some of the jelly and another thin layer of frosting. Add the final sponge layer.

Mask the top and sides of the cake with the remaining mango frosting. For full instructions, see pages 152 to 153.

TO DECORATE
Top the cake with the remaining passion fruit jelly. If the jelly cracks as you transfer it to the cake, you can smooth it using a blowtorch. Press the toasted coconut shavings around the sides of the cake.

If stored in the refrigerator, this cake will last for up to 5 days; however it tastes best if consumed within 3 days. Serve at room temperature.

CHOCOLATE PRALINE TRUFFLE CAKE

THIS CAKE IS A SHOWSTOPPER, PERFECT FOR CHOCOLATE LOVERS. IT LOOKS IMPRESSIVE, YET IT IS RELATIVELY EASY TO MAKE. THE DESIGN LENDS ITSELF TO ALL SORTS OF OCCASIONS, SUCH AS BIRTHDAYS, WEDDINGS, AND ANNIVERSARIES.

INGREDIENTS

For the chocolate cake
1¼ cups (300 g) butter
5 cups (1 kg) packed light brown sugar
1¾ cups (300 g) semisweet chocolate drops
Scant 2 cups (450 ml) milk
9 medium eggs, beaten
Scant 5⅔ cups (675 g) all-purpose flour
6¾ Tbsp unsweetened cocoa powder
2¼ tsp baking soda
2¼ tsp baking powder
½ tsp salt

For the chocolate ganache
5¾ cups (1 kg) semisweet Belgian chocolate drops
(53% cocoa solids)
3 cups (750 ml) whipping cream
Generous ¼ cup (100 g) glucose

For the meringue buttercream
1⅓ cups (270 g) superfine sugar
¼ cup (67 ml) water
4¾ oz (135 g) egg whites, fresh or pasteurized
1½ cups (330 g) butter, softened

For the praline filling
1¼ lb (600 g) chocolate ganache
1 lb 10 oz (750 g) meringue buttercream
¾ cup (150 g) superfine sugar
2 cups (300 g) hazelnuts, toasted

For the decoration
6½ to 9 lb (3 to 4 kg/300 to 400) praline chocolate truffles

EQUIPMENT

Baking tool kit (see page 8)
Layering tool kit (see page 8)
Three 6-in (15-cm) and three 8-in (20-cm) round Sandwich pans
Baking sheet
Small food processor or blender
4 cake dowels
One 6-in (15-cm) and one 8-cm (20-cm) round cake card

Makes one 6-in (15-cm) and one 8-in (20-cm) round cake tier,
serving 60 finger slices or 30 dessert portions.

METHOD

Make the chocolate cake one day ahead.

TO MAKE THE CHOCOLATE CAKE
Preheat the oven to 325°F (160°C).

Line three 6-in (15-cm) and three 8-in (20-cm) sandwich pans with oil spray and wax paper.

Place the butter and half the brown sugar in an electric mixer and, using the paddle, beat at medium-high speed until pale and fluffy.

Meanwhile, place the chocolate drops, milk, and remaining sugar in a deep pan and bring to a boil, stirring occasionally. When the butter and sugar mixture has turned pale and fluffy, slowly add the eggs.

Sift together the flour, cocoa powder, baking soda, baking powder, and salt and add to the mixture, with the mixer set on slow speed.

Pour the hot chocolate mixture into a pitcher and slowly pour it into the cake batter, still mixing on slow speed. Take care, as it could splash.

Once combined, pour the hot cake batter into the prepared pans. Bake for 20 to 30 minutes. The sponge is cooked when it springs back to the touch and the sides are starting to come away from the edges of the pan. If you insert a knife or wooden skewer, it should come out a bit sticky as the texture should be slightly gooey.

Once cooked, let the cakes rest in the pan for about 10 minutes, then transfer to a wire rack to cool.

Wrap the sponges in plastic wrap and let rest overnight at room temperature. This will ensure that all the moisture is sealed and the sponges are a good firm texture for trimming and layering.

TO MAKE THE PRALINE FILLING
Make the chocolate ganache following the instructions on page 13 (using the amounts given on page 76), then let cool to room temperature.

Make the meringue buttercream following the instructions on page 10 and let cool to room temperature.

Put the sugar in a saucepan over medium heat and stir gently until caramelized.

Place the toasted hazelnuts on a lined baking sheet. Pour the caramelized sugar over the top and let cool and set. Smash the praline into pieces, then grind in a food processor until the texture resembles rough sand.

Gently fold 1¼lb (600g) ganache into 1lb 10oz (750g) buttercream and combine. Take care not to overwork the mixture as it can split. Fold through the praline.

TO ASSEMBLE THE CAKE
Trim the six sponge layers and sandwich together using the praline filling, so you have one 6-in (15-cm) cake and one 8-in (20-cm) cake. See pages 150 to 151 for instructions on how to trim and layer the cakes.

Place each cake on a turntable and, using the remaining ganache, mask the top and sides of the cakes (pages 152 to 153). Chill until set.

Trim the 4 cake dowels so they are the same height as the 8-in (20-cm) cake, and push them into the cake in a square formation, as close to the outside as possible but so that they will fit underneath the top tier.

Spread a little ganache in the middle and center the 6-in (15-cm) cake tier on top.

TO DECORATE THE CAKE
Using a large step palette knife, transfer the cake to a cake stand or serving platter. If you are transporting the cake to a venue, place it on a cake drum that is at least 3 in (8 cm) larger than the bottom tier.

Trim each truffle to make a flat surface. Pour the remaining ganache into a pastry bag and use it to stick the truffles onto the cake (the flattened side should sit against the cake). Start by making a row around the bottom and work your way up. (See overleaf, pictures 1 to 4.) Should the ganache be too firm to pipe, warm it in a microwave until soft but not runny.

Store the cake in the refrigerator if not serving immediately. Serve at room temperature. Keep away from heat and direct sunlight. The cake tastes best if consumed within 3 days of baking, but will last for up to 1 week if stored in the refrigerator.

MAPLE AND WALNUT CAKE

THIS IS A LOVELY SUBTLE CAKE WITH A DENSE NUTTY TEXTURE, ABSORBING THE OOZY MAPLE SYRUP PERFECTLY. THE TREE-TRUNK BUTTERCREAM DECORATION PROVIDES A QUIRKY RUSTIC TWIST. ADD MARZIPAN LEAVES AND ACORNS TO COMPLETE THE LOOK.

INGREDIENTS

For the walnut sponge
4 eggs
1¼ cups (150 g) powdered sugar
⅝ cup (150 g) butter, melted
½ cup (120 ml) milk
1½ cups (175 g) all-purpose flour
1 Tbsp baking powder
A pinch of salt
1⅓ cups (125 g) ground almonds
1 cup (100 g) walnuts, toasted and finely chopped

For the maple sugar syrup
⅝ cup (150 ml) water
¾ cup (150 g) sugar
⅓ cup (100 ml) maple syrup

For the maple frosting
1 cup (250 g) whole cream cheese, slightly softened
Generous 1 cup (250 g) unsalted butter, softened
5¼ cups (625 g) powdered sugar, sifted
4 Tbsp dark maple syrup

For the decoration
Acorns and maple leaves made from marzipan

EQUIPMENT

Baking tool kit (see page 8)
Layering tool kit (see page 8)
Three 6-in (15-cm) round sandwich pans
Side scraper with a fine comb patterned edge

Makes one 6-in (15-cm) round cake, serving 8 generous slices.

METHOD

Make the sponge one day ahead.

TO MAKE THE WALNUT SPONGE
Preheat the oven to 347°F (175°C).

Line three 6-in (15-cm) sandwich pans with oil spray and wax paper.

Place the eggs and powdered sugar in an electric mixer and, using the paddle, beat at medium-high speed until pale and fluffy.

Add the butter and milk, beating at medium speed.

In a separate bowl, sift the flour, baking powder, and salt, then fold into the mixture.

Fold in the almonds and walnuts, then transfer the batter to the lined pans.

Bake for 20 to 25 minutes. The sponge is cooked when it springs back to the touch and the sides are coming away from the edges of the pan. If you insert a clean knife into the center, it should come out clean.

While the sponges are baking, make the sugar syrup following the instructions on page 13 and adding the maple syrup.

When the sponges are baked, remove from the oven and let them rest for about 10 minutes. Brush the tops of the sponges with maple sugar syrup (setting aside some for the assembling stage and storing it in the refrigerator overnight).

Once just warm, run a knife all the way around the sides of the pans, remove the sponges, and let cool completely on a wire rack.

Wrap the cooled sponges in plastic wrap and let rest overnight at room temperature. This will ensure that all the moisture is sealed and the sponges firm up to the perfect texture for trimming and layering.

TO MAKE THE MAPLE FROSTING
Make some cream-cheese frosting following the instructions on page 12.

Gently fold in the maple syrup, then refrigerate for at least 2 hours, or until set.

TO ASSEMBLE THE CAKE
Trim the three sponge layers and soak the tops with more maple sugar syrup. Sandwich the layers together using the maple frosting. See pages 150 to 151 for instructions on trimming and layering your cake.

Mask the top and sides of the cake with the remaining maple frosting (pages 152 to 153).

TO DECORATE
While the final layer of frosting is still soft, using a side scraper with a fine patterned edge, scrape the sides of the cake in a vertical motion all around to create a tree-trunk effect.

To mark the top, gently push the tip of a palette knife into the middle of the cake and slowly spin the turntable. Gradually move the palette knife toward the outside as you spin, until you reach the edge.

Decorate the cake with marzipan acorns and leaves, and serve with maple syrup.

If stored in the refrigerator, this cake has a shelf life of up to 5 days; however, it tastes best if consumed within 3 days of baking. Serve at room temperature.

TIRAMISU CAKE

THIS IS A DELICIOUS AFTER-DINNER CAKE OR BIRTHDAY CAKE FOR GENTS. IT LOOKS ATTRACTIVE INSIDE AND OUT, AS IT REVEALS THE LAYERS OF COFFEE, BUTTERCREAM, AND SPONGE WHEN YOU SLICE INTO IT.

INGREDIENTS

For the coffee sponge
2¾ cups (600 g) salted butter
3 cups (600 g) superfine sugar
1 Tbsp vanilla extract
12 medium eggs, room temperature
5 cups (600 g) self-rising flour, sifted
2 Tbsp espresso or strong instant coffee

For the coffee syrup
1 cup (250 ml) water
1¼ cups (250 g) superfine sugar
7 Tbsp (100 ml) espresso or strong instant coffee
Marsala liqueur, to taste

For the mascarpone frosting
7 Tbsp (100 g) unsalted butter, softened
2 cups (250 g) powdered sugar, sifted
⅔ cup (150 g) mascarpone, slightly softened

For the coffee buttercream
2¼ cups (500 g) unsalted butter, softened
Scant 4¼ cups (500 g) powdered sugar, sifted
A pinch of salt
1 Tbsp espresso or strong instant coffee

For the decoration
About 3 Tbsp unsweetened cocoa powder
Coffee buttercream
12 to 16 chocolate coffee beans

EQUIPMENT

Baking tool kit (see page 8)
Layering tool kit (see page 8)
Three 10-in (25-cm) round sandwich pans
Ridged side scraper
Pastry bag
Medium star piping tip

Makes one 10-in (25-cm) cake, serving 12 to 16 generous slices.

METHOD

Make the sponge one day ahead.

TO MAKE THE COFFEE SPONGE
Preheat the oven to 347°F (175°C).

Line three 10-in (25-cm) sandwich pans with oil spray and wax paper.

Place the butter, superfine sugar, and vanilla in an electric mixer and, using the paddle, beat at medium-high speed until pale and fluffy.

Lightly beat the eggs in a separate bowl or pitcher and, with the mixer set on medium speed, slowly pour the eggs into the mixture. If it starts to curdle, add 1 Tbsp of flour to bring it back together.

Once the butter, sugar, and eggs are combined, add the flour and espresso, mixing at low speed, until it is just incorporated.

Using the rubber spatula, fold through the batter to make sure everything is well combined.

Transfer the batter to the lined pans and gently spread it toward the edges with a step palette knife. The batter should be higher around the edges of the pan than in the center, to ensure an even the cake bakes evenly and the height is level.

Bake for 25 to 30 minutes. The sponge is cooked when it springs back to the touch and the sides are coming away from the edges of the pan. If you insert a clean knife into the middle of the sponge, it should come out clean.

While the sponges are baking, make the sugar syrup as shown on page 13 and flavor with the espresso or instant coffee. Once cool, add the liqueur to taste.

When the sponges are baked, remove from the oven and let them rest for about 10 minutes. Brush the tops of the sponges with coffee syrup (setting aside some for the assembling stage and storing it in the refrigerator overnight).

Once just warm, run a knife all the way around the sides of the pans, remove the sponges, and let cool completely on a wire rack.

Wrap the cooled sponges in plastic wrap and let rest overnight at room temperature. This will ensure that all the moisture is sealed so the sponges firm up to the perfect texture for trimming and layering.

TO MAKE THE MASCARPONE FROSTING
Follow the instructions on page 12 using the amounts on page 86 and chill until set.

TO MAKE THE COFFEE BUTTERCREAM
Follow the instructions for English buttercream on page 10, using the amounts on page 86. Gently fold in the coffee and mix well. Let chill until set.

TO ASSEMBLE THE CAKE
Trim the three sponge layers and soak the tops with more coffee syrup. Spread mascarpone frosting over each layer and dust with cocoa powder before placing the next sponge on top. For instructions on trimming and layering your cake, see pages 150 to 151.

Mask the top and sides of the cake with coffee buttercream (pages 152 to 153).

TO DECORATE
Place the cake on a turntable.

Cover the chilled cake with another generous layer of buttercream and, using a ridged side scraper, create a sculptured barrel design (see overleaf, steps 1 to 2).

Chill the cake again until set (about 1 hour).

Dust the top of the cake liberally with cocoa powder (step 3).

Make a two-tone buttercream by mixing 1 Tbsp of coffee buttercream with 1 tsp of cocoa powder. Spread a thin line around the inside of the pastry bag (step 4), then fill the bag with the remaining lighter coffee buttercream (steps 5 to 7).

Pipe small rosettes around the top of the cake (steps 8 to 9) and top each one with a chocolate coffee bean. Store the cake in the refrigerator if not serving immediately and serve at room temperature. This cake tastes best if consumed within 3 days of baking, but will last for 1 week if stored in the refrigerator.

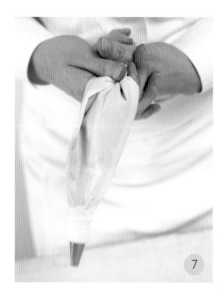

LOVELY LAYER CAKES

CITRUS CAKE

THIS IS A REFRESHING SUMMERY PARTY CAKE BASED ON A SIMPLE VICTORIA SPONGE. YOU CAN COMBINE ANY CITRUS ZESTS—I USED LIME, LEMON, AND ORANGE FOR MY SPONGE AND PINK GRAPEFRUIT TO FLAVOR THE FROSTING. I FIND THIS BITTERSWEET AND ZESTY COMBINATION PARTICULAR TASTY.

INGREDIENTS

For the citrus sponge
Generous 1¾ cups (400 g) butter
2 cups (400 g) superfine sugar
Finely grated zest of 2 oranges, 2 lemons, and 2 limes (set aside the juice for the syrup)
8 medium eggs, room temperature
3⅓ cups (400 g) self-rising flour, sifted

For the citrus syrup
1 cup (200 g) superfine sugar
Juice of 2 oranges, 2 lemons, and 2 limes

For the pink-grapefruit frosting
1⅔ cups (375 g) whole cream cheese, slightly softened
1¾ cups (375 g) unsalted butter, softened
Scant 8 cups (950 g) powdered sugar, sifted
Zest of 2 unwaxed pink grapefruits
Peach food paste color

For the buttercream decoration
Scant 1¼ cups (300 g) butter
2½ cups (300 g) powdered sugar
Peach, yellow, and green food paste color

EQUIPMENT

Baking tool kit (see page 8)
Layering tool kit (see page 8)
Three 8-in (20-cm) round sandwich pans
Fine grater
3 pastry bags
3 large open star piping tips
(You could get away with using just one tip and pastry bag, but it will take a bit longer as you will need to wash them between each use)

Makes one 8-in (20-cm) cake, serving 12 generous slices.

METHOD

Make the sponge one day ahead.

TO MAKE THE CITRUS SPONGE

Preheat the oven to 347°F (175°C).

Line three 8-in (20-cm) sandwich pans with oil spray and wax paper.

Place the butter, superfine sugar, and orange, lemon, and lime zests in an electric mixer and, using the paddle, beat at medium-high speed until pale and fluffy.

Lightly beat the eggs in a separate bowl or pitcher and, with the mixer set at medium speed, slowly pour into the butter mixture. If it starts to curdle, add 1 Tbsp of flour to bring it back together.

Once the butter, sugar, and eggs are combined, mix the flour at low speed until it is just incorporated.

Using a rubber spatula, fold through the batter to make sure everything is well combined.

Transfer the batter to the lined pans and gently spread it toward the edges with a step palette knife. The batter should be higher around the edges than in the center, to ensure the cake bakes evenly and the height is level.

Bake for 20 to 25 minutes. The sponge is cooked when it springs back to the touch and the sides are coming away from the edges of the pan. Alternatively, insert a clean knife into the middle of the sponge; if it is cooked, the knife will come out clean.

While the cake is baking, make the citrus syrup. Put the sugar and citrus juices in a medium saucepan, bring to a boil, then let cool.

Once the sponges are baked, remove from the oven and let rest for about 10 minutes. Brush the tops of the sponges with citrus syrup (setting aside some for the assembling stage and storing it in the refrigerator overnight).

Run a knife all the way around the sides of the pans, remove the sponges, and let cool completely on a wire rack.

Once cool, wrap the sponges in plastic wrap and let rest overnight at room temperature. This will ensure that all the moisture is sealed and the sponges firm up to the perfect texture for trimming and layering.

TO MAKE THE PINK-GRAPEFRUIT FROSTING

Make some cream-cheese frosting following the instructions on page 12, using the amounts given on page 92 and including the pink-grapefruit zest.

Add a little peach food color to a little frosting, mixing until the color is well incorporated. Stir into the remaining frosting to make a pale peach shade.

Refrigerate until the frosting has set.

TO ASSEMBLE THE CAKE

Trim the three sponge layers and soak the tops with citrus syrup. Sandwich together using the pink-grapefruit frosting. See pages 150 to 151 for trimming and layering instructions.

Mask the top and sides of the cake with the remaining pink grapefruit frosting (pages 152 to 153).

TO DECORATE

Cream together the butter and powdered sugar to make a buttercream, following the instructions for English buttercream on page 10.

Divide the buttercream between 3 small bowls and mix each part with a different food color, so you have pale shades of yellow, peach, and lime green.

Put each batch of buttercream into a pastry bag with a star tip attachment. (If you only have one bag and tip, wash them between each color and start with the palest.)

Pipe stars of different sizes and colors randomly over the top of the cake. For a detailed view of the tip and piping style, see page 155.

Store the cake in the refrigerator if not serving immediately, and serve at room temperature. Keep away from heat and direct sunlight. This cake tastes best if consumed within 3 days of baking, but can last for up to 1 week if stored in the refrigerator.

BERRY BASKET CAKE

THIS IS A DELICIOUSLY LIGHT CAKE, BURSTING WITH BERRY FLAVORS. YOU CAN KEEP THE DECORATION SIMPLE OR PIPE THE SIDES OF THE CAKE WITH BASKET WEAVE. THE HEXAGON SHAPE IS A LITTLE CHALLENGING, BUT YOU COULD MAKE A ROUND CAKE IF YOU PREFER, USING THE QUANTITIES GIVEN HERE.

INGREDIENTS

For the chiffon sponge
11¼ oz (320 g) egg yolks
4½ cups (900 g) superfine sugar
1¼ cups (300 ml) vegetable or sunflower oil
1½lb (660 g) egg whites
A pinch of cream of tartar
A pinch of salt
2½ Tbsp vanilla extract
7½ cups (900 g) all-purpose flour
4¼ Tbsp baking powder
2 cups (480 ml) milk

For the vanilla syrup
Generous 1 cup (250 ml) water
1¼ cups (250 g) superfine sugar
2 Tbsp vanilla extract

For the meringue buttercream
5½ cups (1.1 kg) superfine sugar
Generous 1 cup (268 ml) water
1 lb 3 oz (540 g) egg whites
6 cups (1.3 kg) butter
Vanilla extract, to taste

For the filling
1 medium jar raspberry jam
1 medium jar blueberry jam
About 2 cartons each of fresh raspberries, blueberries and blackberries
About 1 carton of strawberries

For the decoration
Fresh berries and flowers (make sure they are suitable for direct food contact, i.e. not poisonous or treated with pesticides)

EQUIPMENT

Baking tool kit (see page 8)
Layering tool kit (see page 8)
Two 6-in (15-cm) and two 10-in (25-cm) hexagon cake pans
One 6-in (15-cm) and one 10-in (25-cm) hexagon cake card
4 cake dowels
Pastry bag
Round piping tip no. 3
Medium basket weave piping tip
Pen star piping tip no. 7

Makes one 6-in (15-cm) and one 10-in (25-cm) hexagon cake tier, serving about 30 dessert portions or 80 finger portions.

METHOD

Make the sponge one day ahead.

TO MAKE THE CHIFFON SPONGE

Preheat the oven to 347°F (175°C).

Line the cake pans with oil spray and wax paper.

Whisk the egg yolks with a little of the sugar until pale and fluffy. Slowly add the oil and whisk until thick.

Put the egg whites, cream of tartar, and salt in an electric mixer and, using the whisk attachment, beat at medium-high speed until the mixture forms soft peaks.

With the mixer still running, slowly pour in the remaining sugar and beat until the mixture is glossy and holds stiff peaks. Beat in the vanilla extract.

In a medium bowl, sift together the flour and baking powder and gradually add to the egg-yolk mixture, gently folding after each addition. Add the milk and fold in the stiff egg whites.

Transfer the batter to the lined pans and gently spread it toward the edges with a step palette knife. The batter should be higher around the edges than in the middle, to ensure an even bake and level cake height.

Bake for 25 to 30 minutes. The sponges are cooked when they spring back to the touch and the sides are coming away from the edges of the pan.

While the sponges are baking, make the sugar syrup following the instructions on page 13, using the amounts on page 96, and add vanilla extract to taste.

When the sponges are baked, remove from the oven and let them rest for about 10 minutes. Brush the tops of the sponges with vanilla syrup (setting aside some for the assembling stage and storing it in the refrigerator overnight).

Transfer the sponges to a wire rack to cool completely, then wrap them in plastic wrap and rest overnight at room temperature.

TO MAKE THE MERINGUE BUTTERCREAM

Follow the instructions on page 10, using the amounts given on page 96, then add vanilla extract to taste.

TO ASSEMBLE THE CAKE

Trim the sponges and slice each one in half horizontally, so you have 4 layers for each tier. Soak each sponge layer with vanilla syrup, then spread the fillings on top, using raspberry jam for the first layer, meringue buttercream, and fresh berries for the second and blueberry jam for the third. See pages 150 to 151 for trimming and layering instructions.

Mask the top and sides of the cake with the remaining meringue buttercream (pages 152 to 153). Keep the corners as sharp and straight as possible.

Trim the 4 dowels to the same height as the bottom tier and push them into the center of the cake in a square formation. They should be as far apart as possible, but within the diameter of the tier above.

Spread more buttercream between the dowels and center the second tier on top. Pipe buttercream into the gap between the tiers, then run your finger along the edge to give it a smooth finish.

TO DECORATE

Place the cake on a turntable with a 12-in (30-cm) cake disk. Put the remaining meringue buttercream in a pastry bag fitted with the round tip.

Starting with the top tier, pipe vertical lines down each side of the cake, first in the middle, then on the corners, then at ½-in (1-cm) intervals in between.

Fit the pastry bag with the basket weave tip and, starting at the bottom, pipe a row of strips over every other line. Repeat on the next row, working in between the strips on the first row.

Once the cake is covered with the basket weave effect, attach the star tip to the pastry bag and pipe a rope border along the top edge of each tier. (See page 155 for detailed images of these piping effects.)

Refrigerate for about 1 hour, then transfer the cake to a serving platter or cake stand using a large step palette knife. Arrange fresh berries and flowers in two clusters on the top and side of the cake.

If stored in the refrigerator, this cake will last for up to 3 days. Serve at room temperature.

GINGERBREAD CAKE

THIS IS A FANTASTIC CAKE TO SHARE WITH FAMILY AND FRIENDS DURING THE FESTIVE SEASON. IT IS LOVELY AND SPICY AND IS TOPPED WITH SCRUMPTIOUS LEMON FROSTING. I DECORATE MINE WITH CUTE LITTLE GINGERBREAD MEN, BUT YOU CAN USE ANY COOKIE SHAPES—THIS CAKE INVITES YOU TO BE CREATIVE AND HAVE FUN.

INGREDIENTS

For the sponge
About 1 cup (250 ml) whole milk

Finely grated zest and juice of 1 unwaxed orange

¾ cup (150 g) packed dark brown sugar

A pinch of salt

Generous ¾ cup (300 g) light corn syrup

Scant ½ cup (150 g) blackstrap molasses

4 tsp ground ginger

4 tsp ground cinnamon

2 tsp ground allspice

Generous ¾ cup (180 g) unsalted butter, chilled, and cut into pieces

3 cups (350 g) self-rising flour

1 tsp baking soda

3 medium eggs, beaten

For the sugar syrup
⅝ cup (150 ml) water

¾ cup (150 g) superfine sugar

For the lemon cream-cheese frosting
1 cup (250 g) whole cream cheese, slightly softened

Generous 1 cup (250 g) unsalted butter, softened

5¼ cups (625 g) powdered sugar, sifted

Finely grated zest of 2 unwaxed lemons

For the decoration
About 8 gingerbread men
(you can buy these or make your own)

A little royal icing
(if making your own gingerbread)

EQUIPMENT

Baking tool kit (see page 8)

Layering tool kit (see page 8)

Three 6-in (15-cm) round sandwich pans

Small gingerbread cookie cutter (if making your own gingerbread)

Paper pastry bag (if decorating your own gingerbread)

Pastry bag

Medium round piping tip

Makes one 6-in (15-cm) round cake, serving 8 generous slices.

METHOD
Make the sponge one day ahead.

TO MAKE THE GINGERBREAD SPONGE
Preheat the oven to 347°F (175°C).

Line three 6-in (15-cm) sandwich pans with oil spray and wax paper.

Add enough milk to the orange juice to make up 1¼ cups (300 ml) of liquid. Place the milk mixture in a saucepan with the zest, sugar, salt, corn syrup, molasses, and spices and gently bring to a boil, stirring constantly.

Remove from the heat and add the butter, stirring with a whisk until melted.

Sift the flour and baking soda into a large bowl and add the slightly cooled liquid mixture. Stir gently with a whisk.

Gradually add the beaten egg and stir through until the cake batter is just smooth and thoroughly combined.

Pour the batter into a pitcher, then transfer to the prepared pans.

Bake for 25 to 30 minutes. The sponge is cooked when it springs back to the touch and the sides are coming away from the edges of the pan. If you insert a clean knife into the middle of the sponge, it should come out clean.

While the sponges are in the oven, make the sugar syrup following the instructions on page 13.

Once the sponges are baked, remove from the oven and let them rest for about 10 minutes. Brush the tops of the sponges with sugar syrup.

Once just warm, run a knife all the way around the sides of the pans, transfer the sponges to a wire rack, and let cool completely.

Once cool, wrap the sponges in plastic wrap and let them rest overnight at room temperature. This will ensure that all the moisture is sealed and the sponges are a good firm texture for trimming and layering.

TO MAKE THE LEMON FROSTING
Make some cream-cheese frosting following the instructions on page 12, then add the lemon zest.

Chill for at least 2 hours, or until set.

TO ASSEMBLE THE CAKE
Trim the three sponge layers, then sandwich them together using lemon frosting. See pages 150 to 151 for instructions on trimming and layering your cake.

Mask the top and sides of the cake with lemon frosting (pages 152 to 153).

TO DECORATE THE CAKE
If you have made your own gingerbread men, fill a paper pastry bag with royal icing, snip off the tip to make a small hole, then pipe on faces and buttons.

Put the remaining lemon frosting into a pastry bag with a medium round tip attached and pipe 8 blobs of frosting evenly around the edge of the cake.

Place a gingerbread man on top of each blob, facing toward the center of the cake.

This cake has a shelf life of up to 1 week if stored in the refrigerator. Serve at room temperature.

SUGAR PLUM CAKE

· ·

THIS DELICIOUS FALL CAKE IS SMARTLY DECORATED WITH OMBRÉ BUTTERCREAM
STRIPES AND TOPPED WITH A CROWN OF GOLDEN PLUMS.

INGREDIENTS

For the cinnamon sponge
⁷⁄₈ cup (200 g) butter
I cup (200 g) superfine sugar
I tsp vanilla extract
4 medium eggs
I²⁄₃ cups (200 g) self-rising flour, sifted
I tsp ground cinnamon
A pinch of salt

For the cinnamon syrup
⁵⁄₈ cup (150 ml) water
¾ cup (150 g) superfine sugar
I cinnamon stick

For the filling
½ cup (200 g) plum jam

For the cinnamon buttercream
2¼ cups (500 g) unsalted butter, softened
Scant 4¼ cups (500 g) powdered sugar, sifted
A pinch of salt
I Tbsp ground cinnamon, sifted
A little purple and pink food paste color

For the decoration
2 fresh plums, pitted and quartered

EQUIPMENT

Baking tool kit (see page 8)
Layering tool kit (see page 8)
Three 6-in (15-cm) round sandwich pans
3 petal piping tips (I used Wilton 104)
3 pastry bags
(You can get away with just one tip and pastry bag,
but it will take a bit longer as you need to wash them
between each use)
Medium round piping tip

Makes one 6-in (15-cm) cake, serving 8 generous slices.

METHOD

Make the sponge one day ahead.

TO MAKE THE CINNAMON SPONGE

Preheat the oven to 347°F (175°C) and line the sandwich pans with oil spray and wax paper.

Place the butter, superfine sugar, and vanilla in an electric mixer and, using the paddle, beat at medium-high speed until pale and fluffy.

Lightly beat the eggs in a separate bowl or pitcher and, with the mixer set at medium speed, slowly pour into the butter mixture. If it starts to curdle, add 1 Tbsp of flour to bring it back together.

Sift together the flour, cinnamon, and salt, add to the mixture, and beat at low speed until just combined. Using a rubber spatula, fold through the batter to make sure everything is well combined.

Transfer the batter to the lined pans and gently spread toward the edges with a step palette knife. The batter should be higher around the edges of the pans than in the center, to ensure an even bake and level height.

Bake for 20 to 25 minutes. The sponges are cooked when they spring back to the touch and the sides are coming away from the edges of the pan. If you insert a clean knife into the middle of the sponge, it should come out clean.

While the sponges are baking, make the cinnamon sugar syrup following the instructions on page 13. When lukewarm, add the cinnamon stick. Remove once the syrup has cooled.

When the sponges are baked, remove from the oven and let rest for about 10 minutes. Brush the tops with cinnamon syrup (setting aside some for the assembling stage and storing it in the refrigerator overnight).

Once just warm, run a knife all the way around the sides of the pans, transfer the sponges to a wire rack, and let cool completely.

Wrap the cooled sponges in plastic wrap and rest overnight at room temperature. This will seal in all the moisture and ensure that the sponges are a good firm texture for trimming and layering.

TO MAKE THE CINNAMON BUTTERCREAM

Make some English buttercream following the instructions on page 10, using the amounts given on page 105. Add the cinnamon and purple food color and mix to a light shade of purple.

TO ASSEMBLE THE CAKE

Trim the three sponge layers and soak the tops with more cinnamon syrup. Sandwich together using the plum jam. See pages 150 to 151 for instructions on trimming and layering the cake.

Place the cake on a turntable and mask the top and sides with the purple buttercream (pages 152 to 153). Apply two layers, or until there is no crumb visible. Chill until set.

TO DECORATE

Divide the remaining buttercream evenly between 3 bowls. Keep one batch in its original color (the middle shade), then add more purple to the second batch to make it darker and a small amount of pink to the third to make it lighter.

Put each batch of buttercream into a pastry bag with a petal tip attached. (If you only have one bag and tip, start with the darkest shade and wash them before adding the middle shade.)

Apply the darkest buttercream first, piping 3 to 4 rows around the bottom of the cake, then repeat with the middle then lightest shade, moving up the sides. You should end up with three even stripes of buttercream around the cake. (See overleaf, steps 1 to 2.)

Use the side scraper to smooth the buttercream, rotating the turntable as you work. You should end up with an ombré effect (steps 3 to 4).

Put the remaining dark purple buttercream in a pastry bag fitted with a round tip and pipe 8 swirls evenly around the top of the cake. Top each swirl with a fresh plum quarter. Store in the refrigerator if not serving immediately and serve at room temperature. Keep away from heat or direct sunlight. This cake tastes best if consumed within 3 days of baking, but lasts for up to 1 week if stored in the fridge.

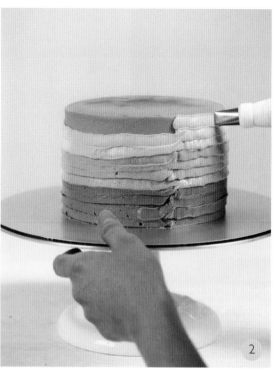

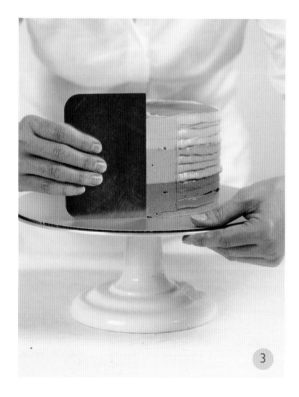

SPICED PUMPKIN CAKE

THIS IS A GREAT CAKE FOR THE FALL SEASON, PERFECT TO CELEBRATE THANKSGIVING OR HALLOWEEN. IT HAS A MOIST AND DENSE TEXTURE YET IT TASTES LIGHT, CREAMY, AND SPICY. I MADE MY OWN PUMPKIN DECORATIONS FROM MARZIPAN, BUT YOU COULD BUY THESE.

INGREDIENTS

For the pumpkin sponge
7 Tbsp (100 g) butter
10 oz (280 g) pumpkin puree
½ teaspoon fine sea salt
½ cup (115 ml) buttermilk
1⅔ cups (325 g) packed light brown sugar
4 eggs
2 cups (240 g) all-purpose flour
2½ tsp baking powder
½ tsp baking soda
¾ tsp ground ginger
1 tsp ground cinnamon
¾ tsp ground nutmeg
¼ tsp ground cloves

For the cinnamon frosting
1 cup (250 g) whole cream cheese, slightly softened
Generous 1 cup (250 g) unsalted butter, softened
5¼ cups (625 g) powdered sugar, sifted
1 Tbsp ground cinnamon

For the decoration
Marzipan pumpkins (bought or homemade)

EQUIPMENT

Baking tool kit (see page 8)
Layering tool kit (see page 8)
Three 6-in (15-cm) round sandwich pans
Patterned side scraper

Makes one 6-in (15-cm) cake, serving 8 generous portions.

METHOD

Make the sponge one day ahead.

TO MAKE THE PUMPKIN SPONGE

Preheat the oven to 344°F (170°C).

Line three 6-in (15-cm) round sandwich pans with oil spray and wax paper.

Melt the butter and let cool slightly. Put the pumpkin puree, salt, buttermilk, and sugar in the large bowl of an electric mixer and, using the whisk attachment, mix well.

Add the eggs gradually, whisking well between each addition.

Sift together the flour, baking powder, baking soda, and spices. Lightly whisk the flour mix into the pumpkin mixture in two batches. Add the melted butter and gently incorporate until just mixed.

Carefully pour the batter into the prepared cake pans and bake for 20 to 25 minutes or until the sponges spring back when gently prodded and an inserted skewer comes out clean.

Remove the cakes from the oven and let rest for about 10 minutes. Once just warm, run a knife all the way around the sides of the pans, remove the sponges, and let cool completely on a wire rack.

Wrap the sponges in plastic wrap and let them rest overnight at room temperature. This will ensure that all the moisture is sealed and the sponges firm up to the perfect texture for trimming and layering.

TO MAKE THE CINNAMON FROSTING

Make some cream-cheese frosting following the instructions on page 12.

Gently fold in the ground cinnamon and chill for at least 2 hours, or until set.

TO ASSEMBLE THE CAKE

Trim the three sponge layers and sandwich them together using the cinnamon frosting. (See pages 150 to 151 for instructions on trimming and layering your cake.)

Mask the top and sides of the cake with the remaining cinnamon frosting (pages 152 to 153).

TO DECORATE

Mask the chilled cake again, using a generous layer of cinnamon frosting. Use a side scraper with a patterned edge to go around the sides of the cake. See the Tiramisu Cake on pages 86 to 91 for a similar method, with detailed images.

Chill again until set.

Decorate the top of the cake with marzipan pumpkins.

NEAPOLITAN CAKE

THIS IS A DELICIOUS COMBINATION OF LIGHT CHIFFON SPONGE AND SMOOTH CHOCOLATE MERINGUE BUTTERCREAM. CHIFFON SPONGE NATURALLY HAS A VERY LIGHT COLOR AND LENDS ITSELF PERFECTLY TO THE CREATION OF THESE DIFFERENT SHADES, WHICH ARE CURRENTLY SO POPULAR.

INGREDIENTS

For the chiffon sponge
5¾ oz (160 g) egg yolks
2¼ cups (450 g) superfine sugar
⅝ cup (150 ml) vegetable oil
11½ oz (330 g) egg whites
A pinch of cream of tartar
A pinch of salt
3 Tbsp vanilla extract
3¾ cups (450 g) all-purpose flour
2 Tbsp (30 g) baking powder
1 cup (240 ml) milk
1 Tbsp (15 g) unsweetened cocoa powder, sifted
A little pink food color

For the vanilla syrup
Generous 1 cup (250 ml) water
1¼ cups (250 g) superfine sugar
2 Tbsp vanilla extract

For the meringue buttercream
2¾ cups (540 g) superfine sugar
½ cup (134 ml) water
9½ oz (270 g) egg whites
3 cups (660 g) butter

For the chocolate ganache
2¼ cups (400 g) semisweet Belgian chocolate drops (53% cocoa solids)
1¼ cups (300 ml) whipping cream
1½ Tbsp glucose

For the decoration
Unsweetened cocoa powder
Plain meringue buttercream

EQUIPMENT

Baking tool kit (see page 8)
Layering tool kit (see page 8)
Three 8-in (20-cm) round sandwich pans
Polka dot cake stencil
Pastry bag
Large round piping tip

Makes one 8-in (20-cm) round cake, serving 12 to 16 generous slices.

METHOD

Make the sponge one day ahead.

TO MAKE THE CHIFFON SPONGES
Preheat the oven to 347°F (175°C).

Line three 8-in (20-cm) sandwich pans with oil spray and wax paper.

Place the egg yolks and a little of the sugar in an electric mixer and, using the whisk attachment, beat until pale and fluffy. Add the oil slowly and mix well until thick.

Put the egg whites, cream of tartar, and salt in an electric mixer and, again using the whisk attachment, beat at medium-high speed until the mixture forms soft peaks.

With the mixer still running, slowly pour in the remaining sugar and beat until the mixture is glossy and holds stiff peaks. Beat in the vanilla extract.

Sift the flour and baking powder together into a medium bowl.

Gradually add the flour mixture to the egg-yolk mixture, gently folding after each addition to incorporate. Add the milk and fold in the stiff egg whites.

Gently divide the batter evenly between 3 bowls. Fold the cocoa powder into one batch and the pink food color into another. You should now have one plain batter, one chocolate, and one pink.

Transfer the batter to the lined pans and gently spread it toward the edges with a step palette knife. The batter should be higher around the edges of the pan and lower in the center.

Bake for 25 to 30 minutes. Insert a clean knife into the middle of each sponge; if they are cooked, the knife will come out clean.

While baking, make some sugar syrup following the instructions on page 13, using the amounts on page 114, then add the vanilla extract to taste.

When the sponges are baked, remove from the oven and let them rest for about 10 minutes. Brush the tops of the sponges with vanilla syrup (setting aside some for the assembling stage and storing it in the refrigerator overnight).

Once the sponge is just warm, run a knife all the way around the sides of the pans, then transfer the sponges to a wire rack and let cool completely.

Wrap the sponges in plastic wrap and let rest overnight at room temperature.

TO MAKE THE MERINGUE BUTTERCREAM
Follow the instructions on page 10, using the amounts on page 114. Let cool at room temperature.

TO MAKE THE CHOCOLATE GANACHE
Follow the instructions on page 13, using the amounts on page 114. Let cool at room temperature.

TO MAKE THE CHOCOLATE BUTTERCREAM
Set aside about 9 oz (250 g) of the buttercream for the decoration. Gently fold 1½ lb (700 g) chocolate ganache into 2½ lb (1k g 150 g) meringue buttercream, being careful not to overwork as it can split.

TO ASSEMBLE THE CAKE
Trim the sponges and soak with more vanilla syrup. Sandwich the sponges together, with the chocolate at the bottom, the pink in the middle, and the vanilla on the top. Spread a coating of chocolate buttercream between each layer. See pages 150 to 151 for trimming and layering instructions.

Mask the top and the sides of the cake with the remaining chocolate buttercream (pages 152 to 153).

TO DECORATE THE CAKE
Center the polka dot stencil on the top of the chilled cake and dust liberally with the cocoa powder. Carefully remove the stencil.

Put the remaining plain meringue buttercream in a pastry bag fitted with a large round tip and pipe 12 blobs evenly around the outside of the cake.

If stored in the refrigerator, this cake will last for up to 5 days; however, it tastes best if consumed within 3 days of baking. Serve at room temperature.

BLACK FOREST CAKE

DERIVED FROM MY GERMAN HERITAGE, THIS IS A SUMPTUOUS AND BOOZY TAKE ON THE TRADITIONAL "SCHWARZWÄLDER KIRSCHTORTE." I USE GRIOTTINE CHERRIES (MORELLO CHERRIES MARINATED IN KIRSCH LIQUEUR), BUT IF YOU CAN'T FIND THEM YOU CAN SOAK YOUR OWN MORELLO CHERRIES FOR A COUPLE OF DAYS BEFORE USE.

INGREDIENTS

For the chocolate sponge
7 Tbsp (100 g) butter
1¾ cups (340 g) light brown sugar
½ cup (100 g) semisweet chocolate drops
(53% cocoa solids)
⅝ cup (150 ml) milk
3 medium eggs
Scant 2 cups (225 g) all-purpose flour
2¼ Tbsp unsweetened cocoa powder
¾ tsp baking soda
¾ tsp baking powder
A pinch of salt
Griottine cherries, drained (set aside
the syrup for soaking)

For the kirsch frosting
1 cup (250 g) whole cream cheese, slightly softened
Generous 1 cup (250 g) unsalted butter, softened
5¼ cups (625 g) powdered sugar, sifted
1 Tbsp vanilla extract
4 Tbsp kirsch liqueur (or to taste)

For the decoration
Kirsch frosting
Griottine cherries
Chocolate sprinkles

EQUIPMENT

Baking tool kit (see page 8)
Layering tool kit (see page 8)
Three 6-in (15-cm) round sandwich pans
Pastry bag
Medium star piping tip

Makes one 6-in (15-cm) round cake, serving 8 generous slices.

METHOD

Make the sponge one day ahead.

TO MAKE THE CHOCOLATE SPONGE
Preheat the oven to 325°F (160°C).

Line three 6-in (15-cm) sandwich pans with oil spray and wax paper.

Place the butter and half the sugar in an electric mixer and, using the paddle attachment, beat at medium-high speed until pale and fluffy.

Meanwhile, put the chocolate, milk, and remaining sugar in a deep saucepan and bring to a boil, stirring occasionally.

When the butter and sugar is pale and fluffy, slowly add the eggs.

Sift together the flour, cocoa powder, baking soda, baking powder, and salt and add to the mixture while beating at slow speed.

Pour the hot chocolate mixture into a pitcher and slowly pour it into the cake batter while mixing on slow speed. Take care, as the hot mixture could splash.

Once combined, pour the hot cake batter into the prepared pans. Drop a handful of the cherries into each pan.

Bake for 20 to 25 minutes. The sponge is cooked when it springs back to the touch and the sides are coming away from the edges of the pan. If you insert a clean knife into the middle of the sponge, it should NOT come out clean but with a small amount of crumb. Be careful not to overbake this cake; it should have a slightly gooey texture.

Once cooked, let the cakes rest for about 10 minutes. Brush the tops with the syrup reserved from the griottine cherries, let cool until just warm, then transfer to a wire rack and let cool completely.

Wrap the sponges in plastic wrap and let them rest overnight at room temperature. This will ensure that all the moisture is sealed and the sponges firm up to the perfect texture for trimming and layering.

TO MAKE THE KIRSCH FROSTING
Make some cream-cheese frosting following the instructions on page 12.

Gently fold through the vanilla extract and kirsch liqueur to taste.

Chill in the refrigerator until set.

TO ASSEMBLE THE CAKE
Trim the three sponge layers and soak the tops with more of the reserved griottine cherry syrup. Sandwich together using kirsch frosting, and sprinkle a handful of griottine cherries evenly over the frosting before placing the next sponge layer on top. See pages 150 to 151 for instructions on how to trim and layer your cake.

Place the cake on a turntable and mask with kirsch frosting (pages 152 to 153).

TO DECORATE
Fill a pastry bag with the remaining kirsch frosting and, using a star tip, pipe 8 rosettes around the outside of the cake.

Top each rosette with a griottine cherry and lightly sprinkle the cake with chocolate.

Store the cake in the refrigerator if not serving immediately. Serve at room temperature. Keep away from heat and direct sunlight. This cake tastes best if consumed within 3 days of baking, but can last for up to 1 week if stored in the refrigerator.

CHEEKY MONKEY CAKE

THIS IS A YUMMY, WHOLESOME CAKE, LOVED NOT ONLY BY CHILDREN BUT BY GROWN-UPS, TOO. IF YOU PREFER NOT TO DECORATE IT WITH CANDIES, USE FRESH BANANA SLICES INSTEAD.

INGREDIENTS

For the banana sponge
1 cup (225 g) butter
2¼ cups (450 g) packed light brown sugar
1 tsp vanilla extract
3 eggs
1¼ lb (600 g) overripe banana, mashed
Scant 1 cup (150 g) chocolate chips, chopped
Generous 3⅓ cups (405 g) all-purpose flour, sifted
2 tsp baking soda
2 tsp white wine vinegar

For the vanilla syrup
⅝ cup (150 ml) water
¾ cup (150 g) superfine sugar
1 Tbsp vanilla extract

For the peanut buttercream
1⅓ cups (270 g) superfine sugar
¼ cup (67 ml) water
4¾ oz (135 g) egg whites
1½ cups (330 g) butter
4 Tbsp peanut butter, smooth

For the decoration
Chocolate sprinkles
Foam banana candies

EQUIPMENT

Baking tool kit (see page 8)
Layering tool kit (see page 8)
Three 6-in (15-cm) round cake pans
Pastry bag
Large star piping tip

Makes one 6-in (15-cm) cake, serving 8 generous slices.

METHOD

Make the sponge one day ahead.

TO MAKE THE BANANA SPONGE
Preheat the oven to 347°F (175°C).

Line three 6-in (15-cm) sandwich pans with oil spray and wax paper.

Place the butter, light brown sugar, and vanilla in an electric mixer and, using the paddle, beat at medium-high speed until pale and fluffy.

Lightly beat the eggs in a separate bowl or pitcher and slowly pour into the butter mixture while paddling on medium speed. If it starts to curdle, add 1 Tbsp of flour to bring it back together.

Once the butter, sugar, and eggs are combined, add the mashed banana and chocolate chips and beat at low speed until just combined.

Add the flour using the rubber spatula, folding through the batter to make sure everything is well combined.

Mix together the baking soda and white wine vinegar and quickly add to the mixture.

Transfer the batter to the lined pans and gently spread it toward the edges with a step palette knife. Bake for 20 to 25 minutes.

The sponge is cooked when it springs back to the touch and the sides are coming away from the edges of the pan. If you insert a clean knife into the middle of the sponge, it should come out clean.

While the sponges are in the oven, cook the sugar syrup following the instructions on page 13. Add the vanilla extract.

Remove the sponges from the oven and let them rest for about 10 minutes. Brush the tops of the sponges with vanilla syrup (setting aside some for the assembling stage and storing it in the refrigerator overnight).

Once just warm, run a knife all the way around the sides of the pans, remove the sponges, and let cool completely on a wire rack.

Wrap the sponges in plastic wrap and let rest overnight at room temperature. This will ensure that all the moisture is sealed and the sponges firm up to the perfect texture for trimming and layering.

TO MAKE THE PEANUT MERINGUE BUTTERCREAM
Make some meringue buttercream following the instructions on page 10.

Gently fold the peanut butter into 1 lb 10 oz (750 g) meringue buttercream.

TO ASSEMBLE THE CAKE
Trim the three sponge layers and soak the tops with vanilla syrup. Sandwich together using the peanut buttercream. See pages 150 to 151 for trimming and layering instructions.

Mask the top and sides of the cake with peanut buttercream (pages 152 to 153).

TO DECORATE
Sprinkle plenty of chocolate sprinkles onto a baking sheet lined with wax paper.

Roll the sides of the chilled cake over the sprinkles, so that you have an even covering. If you prefer, you can apply the sprinkles by hand, holding the cake at an angle.

Fill a pastry bag with the remaining peanut meringue buttercream and, using a star tip, pipe upside-down shell scrolls onto the top of the cake. Top each scroll with a banana candy.

If stored in the refrigerator, this cake will last for up to 5 days; however, it tastes best if consumed within 3 days of baking. Serve at room temperature.

STRAWBERRY AND CHAMPAGNE CAKE

THIS IS A DELECTABLE CAKE, PERFECT FOR A ROMANTIC CELEBRATION. THE GOLD DRAGEES ADD A TOUCH OF GLAMOUR, BUT YOU COULD USE FRESH STRAWBERRIES OR CHAMPAGNE CHOCOLATE TRUFFLES INSTEAD.

INGREDIENTS

For the vanilla sponge
3⅔ cups (800 g) butter
4 cups (800 g) superfine sugar
1 Tbsp vanilla extract
16 medium eggs
6⅔ cups (800 g) self-rising flour, sifted

For the champagne syrup
2 cups (500 ml) water
2½ cups (500 g) superfine sugar
4 Tbsp Marc de champagne
(add to taste)

For the English buttercream
4½ cups (1 kg) unsalted butter, softened
8⅓ cups (1 kg) powdered sugar, sifted
½ tsp salt
A little pink food paste color

For the filling
1¾ cups (600 g) strawberry & champagne preserve

For the decoration
Gold dragees

EQUIPMENT

Baking tool kit (see page 8)
Layering tool kit (see page 8)
Three 4-in (10-cm), three 6-in (15-cm), and three 8-in (20-cm)
round sandwich pans
One 4-in (10-cm), one 6-in (15-cm), and one 8-in (20-cm)
round cake card
5 cake dowels
Pastry bag

Makes one 4-in (10-cm), one 6-in (15-cm), and one 8-in (20-cm) round cake tier.
Serves about 70 finger portions or about 25 dessert slices.

METHOD

Make the sponge one day ahead.

TO MAKE THE VANILLA SPONGES
Preheat the oven to 347°F (175°C).

Line all the sandwich pans with oil spray and wax paper.

Place the butter, superfine sugar, and vanilla in an electric mixer and, using the paddle, beat at medium-high speed until pale and fluffy.

Lightly beat the eggs in a separate bowl or pitcher and, with the mixer set at medium speed, slowly pour into the butter mixture. If it starts to curdle, add 1 Tbsp of flour to bring it back together.

Once the butter, sugar, and eggs are combined, add the flour and mix at low speed until just incorporated. Using the rubber spatula, fold through the batter to make sure everything is well combined.

Transfer the batter to the lined pans and gently spread it toward the edges with a step palette knife. The batter should be higher around the edges than in the middle, to ensure an even bake and level top.

Bake for 20 to 30 minutes. The sponge is cooked when it springs back to the touch and the sides are coming away from the edges of the pan. If you insert a clean knife into the center, it should come out clean.

While the cake is baking, make the sugar syrup following the instructions on page 13, using the amounts given on page 126. Let cool, then add the Marc de Champagne to taste.

Remove the sponges from the oven and rest for 10 minutes. Brush the tops of the sponges with champagne syrup (setting aside some for assembling and storing it in the refrigerator overnight).

Once just warm, remove the sponges from the pans and let cool completely on a wire rack.

Wrap the sponges in plastic wrap and let rest overnight at room temperature. This will seal in all the moisture and ensure that the sponges firm up to the perfect texture for trimming and layering.

TO MAKE THE ENGLISH BUTTERCREAM
Make English buttercream following the instructions on page 10, using the amounts given on page 126. Mix in enough pink food color to make a pale peachy pink.

TO ASSEMBLE THE CAKE
Trim the cakes and soak the tops with champagne syrup, then sandwich the layers together using the strawberry and champagne preserve (see pages 150 to 151 for trimming and layering tips). You should end up with one 4-in (10-cm) cake, one 6-in (15-cm) cake, and one 8-in (20-cm) cake, all the same height.

Place each cake on a turntable and mask with pink buttercream (see pages 152 to 153 for instructions on masking the cakes).

Trim 4 cake dowels to the same height as the 8-in (20-cm) cake tier and 1 dowel to the same height as the 6-in (15-cm) tier (check against the correct tier, just in case there is a slight variation).

Take the 4 trimmed dowels and push them into the center of the 8-in (20-cm) tier in a square formation, as close to the outside as possible without going beyond the circumference of the tier that will sit above. Push the single dowel into the center of the 6-in (15-cm) tier.

Spread a small amount of buttercream around the middle of the 8-in (20-cm) tier and center the 6-in (15-cm) cake on top. Repeat the process on the 6-in (15-cm) tier and place the 4-in (10-cm) cake on top. Make sure that all three tiers are perfectly centered and level.

Put some buttercream in a paper pastry bag, snip off the tip, and use it to fill any gaps between the tiers. Use your little finger to smooth the buttercream and create a neat finish.

TO DECORATE
Pipe a little buttercream onto the gold dragées and stick them around the base of each tier in a random champagne-bubble pattern. Store in the refrigerator if not serving immediately and serve at room temperature. Keep away from heat or direct sunlight. The cake tastes best if eaten within 3 days of baking, but will last up to 1 week if stored in the refrigerator.

S'MORES CAKE

●●

INSPIRED BY THE AMERICAN CAMPFIRE TREAT, THIS CAKE IS MADE FROM A LIGHTLY
SPICED SPONGE, DRENCHED IN HONEY SYRUP, LAYERED WITH CHOCOLATE GANACHE
AND BUTTERCREAM, AND FINISHED WITH BURNED MERINGUE.

INGREDIENTS

For the spiced sponge

½ cup (105 g) butter
1⅓ cups (275 g) packed light brown sugar
1 tsp vanilla extract
2 eggs
2 cups (250 g) all-purpose flour
1 tsp ground cinnamon
A pinch of salt
1 cup (250 ml) buttermilk
1¼ tsp white wine vinegar
1 tsp baking soda

For the honey syrup

½ cup (125 ml) water
⅓ cup (125 ml) honey

For the meringue buttercream

1⅓ cups (270 g) superfine sugar
¼ cup (67 ml) water
4¾ oz (135 g) egg whites
1½ cups (330 g) butter

For the Italian meringue

½ cup (112 g) sugar
3½ Tbsp water
2 egg whites
A pinch of cream of tartar
A pinch of salt

For the chocolate ganache

Scant 1¼ cups (200 g) semisweet Belgian
chocolate drops (53% cocoa solids)
⅝ cup (150 ml) whipping cream
1 Tbsp glucose

EQUIPMENT

Baking tool kit (see page 8)
Layering tool kit (see page 8)
Three 6-in (15-cm) shallow round sandwich pans
Sugar thermometer
Side scraper
Pastry bag
Large round piping tip
Blowtorch

Makes one 6-in (15-cm) round cake, serving 8 generous slices.

METHOD

Make the sponge one day ahead.

TO MAKE THE SPICED SPONGE
Preheat the oven to 347°F (175°C).

Line the three sandwich pans with oil spray and wax paper.

Place the butter, sugar, and vanilla in the bowl of an electric mixer fitted with the paddle, then beat at medium-high speed until pale and fluffy.

Lightly beat the eggs in a separate bowl or pitcher and, with the mixer set at medium speed, slowly pour into the butter mixture. If the mixture starts to curdle, add 1 Tbsp of flour to bring it back together.

Sift the flour, cinnamon, and salt into a bowl. Mixing at low speed, gently add these dry ingredients and the buttermilk in batches.

Mix together the vinegar and baking soda and quickly add to the mixture. Using a rubber spatula, gently fold through the batter to make sure there are no lumps.

Transfer the batter to the pans and gently spread out toward the edges with a step palette knife. Bake for 20 to 25 minutes. The sponge is cooked when it springs back to touch and the sides are coming away from the edges of the pan.

While the sponges are baking, make the honey syrup. Heat the water and honey in a saucepan, stirring regularly, until the honey has dissolved.

Remove the sponges from the oven and let them rest for about 10 minutes. Using a pastry brush, soak the tops with the honey syrup.

Remove the sponges from the pans and let cool completely on a wire rack.

Wrap the sponges in plastic wrap and let rest overnight at room temperature.

TO MAKE THE MERINGUE BUTTERCREAM
Make the meringue buttercream following the instructions on page 10.

TO MAKE THE ITALIAN MERINGUE
Put the sugar and water in a small saucepan over medium-high heat and bring to a boil.

Place the egg whites, cream of tartar, and salt in an electric mixer and, using the whisk attachment, whip at a low speed until frothy.

When the sugar mixture reaches a rapid boil, check the temperature and cook until it reaches 250°F (121°C).

With the mixer running, pour the syrup directly over the meringue in a thin, steady stream, avoiding the whisk and the sides of the bowl. Whip until cool to the touch; this could take a few minutes. The meringue should be shiny and stiff (see overleaf, step 1). Let cool completely.

TO MAKE THE CHOCOLATE GANACHE
Please follow the instructions on page 13.

TO ASSEMBLE THE CAKE
Trim the sponges and soak the tops with more of the honey syrup. Sandwich the sponges together, spreading an even coating of chocolate ganache and a layer of buttercream in between the layers. See pages 150 to 151 for a step-by-step guide to trimming and layering your cake.

Crumb coat the top and sides of the cake (pages 152 to 153) with the remaining meringue buttercream and chill until set.

TO DECORATE
For the final mask, cover the top and sides of the cake with Italian meringue using a palette knife (see overleaf, steps 2 to 3), then use a side scraper to create a smooth finish around the sides (step 4) and the palette knife to level off the top (step 5).

Put the remaining meringue in a pastry bag fitted with a large round tip. Pipe "flames" onto the top of the cake (steps 6 to 7).

Using a blowtorch, lightly brown the sides and the top of the cake (steps 8 to 9). If stored in the refrigerator, this cake will last for up to 3 days. Serve at room temperature.

MAD HATTER'S CHECKERBOARD CAKE

THIS CAKE IS SO INTRIGUING—ALL YOUR GUESTS WILL WONDER HOW YOU CREATED THIS STRIKING CHECKERBOARD PATTERN.

INGREDIENTS

For the vanilla sponge
⅞ cup (200 g) unsalted butter
1 cup (200 g) superfine sugar
1 Tbsp vanilla extract
4 medium eggs, room temperature
1⅔ cups (200 g) self-rising flour, sifted

For the chocolate sponge
7 Tbsp (100 g) unsalted butter
1¾ cups (340 g) light brown sugar
½ cup (100 g) semisweet chocolate drops
⅝ cup (150 ml) milk
3 medium eggs
Scant 2 cups (225 g) all-purpose flour, sifted
2¼ Tbsp unsweetened cocoa powder
¾ tsp baking soda
¾ tsp baking powder
A pinch of salt

For the vanilla syrup
⅝ cup (150 ml) water
¾ cup (150 g) superfine sugar
1 Tbsp vanilla extract (or to taste)

For the buttercream
1⅓ cups (300 g) unsalted butter, softened
2½ cups (300 g) powdered sugar, sifted
A pinch of salt
1 Tbsp vanilla extract

For the decorations
Buttercream
Hydrangea design: green and purple food color
Rosebud design: green and pink food color
Blossom design: yellow food color
Silver sugar pearls

EQUIPMENT

Baking tool kit (see page 8)
Layering tool kit (see page 8)
Four 6-in (15-cm) round sandwich pans
Round dough cutters, about 5-in (12-cm), 3½-in (9-cm),
and 2-in (5-cm) in diameter
Pastry bag
Small crimped star piping tip (hydrangea/rosebud)
Small leaf piping tip (hydrangea/rosebud)
Medium petal piping tip, Wilton 104 (blossom)

Makes one 6-in (15-cm) round cake, serving 8 generous slices.

METHOD

Make the sponge one day ahead.

TO MAKE THE VANILLA SPONGE

Preheat the oven to 347°F (175°C). Line two sandwich pans with oil spray and wax paper.

Put the butter, superfine sugar, and vanilla in an electric mixer and, using the paddle, beat at medium-high speed until pale and fluffy.

Lightly beat the eggs, then slowly pour into the mixer, beating at medium speed. If the mixture curdles, add 1 Tbsp of flour to bring it back together. Once combined, add the flour and mix at low speed until just incorporated. Using a rubber spatula, fold through the batter to make sure everything is combined. Transfer the batter to the lined pans, then bake for 20 to 25 minutes.

While the sponges are baking, make the sugar syrup following the instructions on page 13, using the amounts given on page 136 and adding the vanilla.

Remove the sponges from the oven and let rest for 10 minutes. Using a pastry brush, soak the tops with vanilla syrup, then transfer to a wire rack to cool completely. Wrap the sponges in plastic wrap and let rest overnight at room temperature.

TO MAKE THE CHOCOLATE SPONGE

Preheat the oven to 325°F (160°C). Line two sandwich pans with oil spray and wax paper.

Put the butter and half of the brown sugar in an electric mixer and, using the paddle attachment, beat at medium-high speed until pale and fluffy.

Put the chocolate, milk, and remaining sugar in a deep pan and bring to a boil, stirring occasionally.

Slowly add the eggs to the butter mixture. Sift together the flour, cocoa powder, baking soda, baking powder, and salt. Add to the mixture, beating slowly.

Transfer the hot chocolate mixture to a pitcher and slowly pour into the cake batter while mixing at slow speed. Once combined, pour the hot cake batter into the prepared pans and bake for 20 to 25 minutes.

When the sponges are baked, remove from the oven and let cool and rest as for the vanilla sponges.

TO MAKE THE BUTTERCREAM

Make the English buttercream following the instructions on page 10, using the amounts given on page 136. Fold in the vanilla once the basic ingredients are combined.

TO ASSEMBLE THE PURPLE CAKE

Trim the sponges as shown on pages 150 to 151, step 1. Using the dough cutters, cut each sponge into even rings (see opposite, steps 1 to 2). Alternate the flavors of the cutouts and stick the rings together using a thin layer of piped buttercream (steps 3 to 7).

Sandwich the layers with a thin coating of buttercream (step 8), making sure you alternate the colors (step 9). Put a small amount of buttercream in a bowl, add a little green food color, and mix to a light green.

Mask the top and sides of the cake with buttercream, as shown on pages 152 to 153. Combine the remaining buttercream with a little purple food color to achieve a light purple, and use for the final layer of masking. For the pink or yellow cake, adjust the color accordingly.

TO DECORATE THE PURPLE CAKE

Divide the remaining purple buttercream between two bowls. Add more purple food color to one bowl.

Put the lighter shade into a pastry bag and, using the star tip, pipe small, well-spaced hydrangea blossoms in clusters on the top and sides of the cake. Pipe darker purple blossoms in between the paler ones.

Put the green buttercream into a pastry bag fitted with the leaf tip and pipe leaves around the clusters.

For detailed images of the piping effects used on the cakes shown on pages 138 to 39, see page 154. To recreate the yellow blossoms, pipe the buttercream onto small squares of wax paper, holding the tip rounded side downward in the middle of the paper. As you squeeze the pastry bag, move the tip back and forth, working around until you have a full blossom. Press a sugar pearl into the center. Chill until set, then press onto the cake.

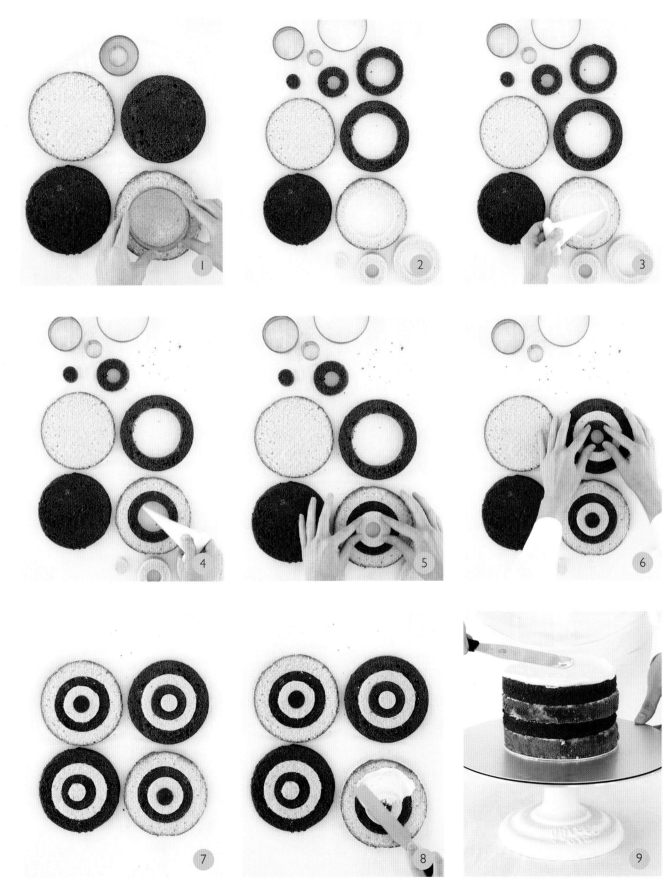

MAD HATTER'S CHECKERBOARD CAKE

PEACH AND ALMOND TORTE

THIS CAKE IS BASED ON A RECIPE FOR ONE OF THE VERY FIRST LAYER CAKES THAT I ATTEMPTED AS A TEENAGER. IT'S A DELICATE ALMOND SPONGE SOAKED WITH GRAND MARNIER SYRUP AND LAYERED WITH CINNAMON BUTTERCREAM AND POACHED PEACHES.

INGREDIENTS

For the almond sponge
⅞ cup (200 g) salted butter
1 cup (200 g) superfine sugar
1 tsp vanilla extract
4 medium eggs, room temperature
1⅔ cups (200 g) self-rising flour, sifted
Generous 1 cup (100 g) ground almonds

For the poached peaches
⅞ cup (200 ml) water
1 cup (200 g) superfine sugar
2 cinnamon sticks
3 fresh peaches, peeled

For the Grand Marnier syrup
Strained poaching liquid
Grand Marnier, to taste

For the cinnamon meringue buttercream
2¾ cups (540 g) superfine sugar
½ cup (134 ml) water
9½ oz (270 g) egg whites
3 cups (660 g) butter
2 Tbsp ground cinnamon, to taste

For the decoration
8 golden sugared almonds
Marzipan peaches (bought or homemade)

EQUIPMENT

Baking tool kit (see page 8)
Layering tool kit (see page 8)
Three 6-in (15-cm) round sandwich pans
Pastry bag
Round piping tip no. 3
For the tiered cake only: 8 cake dowels
One 6-in (15-cm), one 8-in (20-cm), and one 10-in (25-cm) round cake card

Makes a 6-in (15-cm) round cake, serving 8 generous slices.
To recreate the 3-tier cake shown, you will need a 10-in (25-cm), 8-in (20-cm), and 6-in (15-cm) tier. Multiply the amounts by three for a 10-in (25-cm) tier and by two for an 8-in (20-cm) tier.

METHOD

Poach the peaches and make the sponge one day ahead of the cake.

TO POACH THE PEACHES

Put the water, sugar, and cinnamon sticks in a medium saucepan and bring to a simmer.

Put the peaches in the liquid and poach gently for about 15 to 20 minutes, until tender but not soft. Turn the peaches around during poaching and frequently baste with the syrup. Remove from the poaching liquid and let cool.

Bring the poaching liquid to a boil and reduce by half, then add the Grand Marnier according to taste.

TO MAKE THE ALMOND SPONGE

Preheat the oven to 347°F (175°C).

Line three sandwich pans with oil spray and wax paper.

Put the butter, superfine sugar, and vanilla in an electric mixer and, using the paddle, beat at medium-high speed until pale and fluffy.

Lightly beat the eggs and, with the mixer set at medium speed, slowly add to the mixture. If it starts to curdle, add 1 Tbsp of flour.

Once the butter, sugar, and eggs are combined, add the flour and ground almonds and beat at low speed until just incorporated. Using a rubber spatula, fold through the batter to make sure everything is mixed.

Transfer the batter to the lined pans and gently spread toward the edges with a step palette knife. Bake for 20 to 25 minutes.

When the sponges are baked, remove from the oven and let rest for about 10 minutes. Brush the tops of the sponges with Grand Marnier syrup (setting aside some for the assembling stage and storing it in the refrigerator overnight).

Remove the sponges from the pans and let cool completely on a wire rack. Wrap the sponges in plastic wrap and let rest overnight at room temperature.

TO MAKE THE CINNAMON MERINGUE BUTTERCREAM

Make the meringue buttercream following the instructions on page 10, using the amounts given on page 143. Add the ground cinnamon to taste.

TO ASSEMBLE THE CAKE

Slice each peach in half, remove the pit, and cut into thin, even slices.

Trim the sponge layers and soak with Grand Marnier syrup. Spread a thin layer of cinnamon meringue buttercream over each sponge, then arrange peach slices evenly on top, making sure the surface is completely covered. Spread another thin layer of buttercream over the peaches before placing the next sponge layer on top. For trimming and layering instructions, see pages 150 to 151.

Mask the top and sides of the cake with the cinnamon meringue buttercream (pages 152 to 153).

TO DECORATE

Put the remaining meringue buttercream in a pastry bag fitted with the round tip. Pipe a snail trail around the base of the cake. Pipe a row of double swags around the top edge of the cake and place a sugared almond over each join. For detailed images of the piping techniques used here, see page 154.

Decorate the top of the cake with marzipan peaches.

If not serving immediately, store the cake in the refrigerator where it will last for up to 5 days; however, it will taste best if consumed within 3 days of baking. Serve at room temperature.

FOR THE TIERED CAKE

Before you decorate the cake tiers, you will need to dowel and stack them. You will need 4 cake dowels for the bottom tier and 4 for the middle tier. They will prevent the cakes from sinking into each other. Cut the dowels to the same height as the tier and push them into the middle in a square formation, as far apart as possible but not beyond the circumference of the tier that will sit above. Stick the tiers in place using buttercream, and decorate as above.

PIÑA COLADA CAKE

THIS FABULOUS PARTY CAKE IS INSPIRED BY ONE OF MY FAVORITE COCKTAILS.
THE FRAGRANT AROMAS OF COCONUT, FRESH LIME ZEST, AND PINEAPPLE EVOKE
MEMORIES OF HOT SUMMER VACATIONS AT THE BEACH.

INGREDIENTS

For the pineapple flowers

1 fresh pineapple

**For the coconut and
pineapple sponge**

1 cup (225 g) butter

1⅛ cups (225 g) superfine sugar

Zest of 2 unwaxed limes

4 eggs

2 cups (240 g) self-rising flour

Generous 1 cup (100 g) dry unsweetened coconut

5¼ oz (150 g) fresh pineapple, cubed
(set aside from pineapple flowers)

For the malibu syrup

⅝ cup (150 ml) water

¾ cup (150 g) superfine sugar

Malibu liqueur, to taste

For the lime frosting

1 cup (250 g) whole cream cheese,
softened slightly

Generous 1 cup (250 g) unsalted butter, softened

5¼ cups (625 g) powdered sugar, sifted

Zest of 2 unwaxed limes

2 Tbsp Malibu liqueur

EQUIPMENT

Baking tool kit (see page 8)

Layering tool kit (see page 8)

Long carving knife

Paper towels

Three 6-in (15-cm) shallow round sandwich pans

Silicone tray with sphere molds
(see Suppliers on page 156)

Makes one 6-in (15-cm) cake, serving 20 slices.

METHOD

Make the pineapple flowers and sponge one day ahead (make the pineapple flowers first, so you can use the leftover pineapple for the sponge). Assemble the cake on the day.

TO MAKE THE PINEAPPLE FLOWERS

Place the pineapple on a cutting board and cut off the top and bottom. Carefully cut away the skin.

Using a long carving knife, cut waves lengthwise around the sides of the pineapple to form a flower shape.

Slice the pineapple thinly, so you have at least 15 flowers. Dab the flowers with a paper towel to help them to dry out. Place them in a sphere tray, then put them in the oven at 225°F (110°C) for a few hours, until dried out. They should hold their shape.

Let the flowers cool, then immediately wrap them in plastic wrap to keep them crisp.

TO MAKE THE COCONUT AND PINEAPPLE SPONGE

Preheat the oven to 347°F (175°C).

Line three 6-in (15-cm) sandwich pans with oil spray and wax paper.

Place the butter, superfine sugar, and lime zest in an electric mixer and, using the paddle, beat at medium-high speed until pale and fluffy.

Lightly beat the eggs in a separate bowl or pitcher and, with the mixer set at medium speed, slowly pour into the butter mixture. If it starts to curdle, add 1 Tbsp of flour to bring it back together.

Once the butter, sugar, and eggs are combined, add the flour, coconut, and pineapple.

Transfer the batter to the lined pans and gently spread toward the edges with a step palette knife. The batter should be higher around the edges than in the middle, to ensure an even bake and level height.

Bake for 20 to 25 minutes. The sponge is cooked when it springs back to the touch and the sides are coming away from the edges of the pan. A clean knife inserted into the center of the sponge should come out clean.

While the sponges are in the oven, make some sugar syrup following the instructions on page 13. Let cool, then add the Malibu liqueur according to taste.

When the sponges are baked, remove from the oven and let rest for about 10 minutes. Brush the tops of the sponges with Malibu syrup (setting aside some for the assembling stage and storing it in the refrigerator overnight).

Run a knife all the way around the sides of the pans, remove the sponges, and let cool completely on a wire rack.

Wrap the sponges in plastic wrap and let rest overnight at room temperature. This will ensure that all the moisture is sealed and the sponges firm up to the perfect texture for trimming and layering.

TO MAKE THE LIME FROSTING

Make some cream-cheese frosting following the instructions on page 12, then fold in the lime zest and Malibu liqueur.

TO ASSEMBLE THE CAKE

Trim the three sponge layers and soak with Malibu syrup, then sandwich together using the lime frosting. See pages 150 to 151 for instructions on how to trim and layer the cake.

Mask the top and sides of the cake with lime frosting, following the instructions on pages 152 to 153.

TO DECORATE

Just before serving, arrange the pineapple flowers on the top of the cake, attaching them with dabs of cream-cheese frosting. Note that, once exposed to air, the flowers will start to soften and begin to lose their shape.

If stored in the refrigerator, this cake will last for up to 5 days; however, it will taste best if consumed within 3 days of baking. Serve at room temperature.

LAYERING TECHNIQUE

THESE INSTRUCTIONS ARE A GENERAL GUIDE TO TRIMMING AND LAYERING; THE PROCESS WILL VARY SLIGHTLY FROM ONE RECIPE TO ANOTHER. MAKE SURE ALL THE SPONGE LAYERS HAVE COOLED COMPLETELY BEFORE ASSEMBLING. IDEALLY, WRAP THEM IN PLASTIC WRAP AND LET REST OVERNIGHT. ANY BUTTERCREAM, GANACHE, OR OTHER FILLINGS SHOULD BE SPREADABLE. ENSURE THAT THEY ARE ROOM TEMPERATURE BEFORE USE.

1 Using a bread knife or cake leveler, trim the top crust off each sponge. For the middle layer (or layers), also trim off the browned base of the sponge. Aim to make all the sponges the same depth—to help with this, I use a ruler when adjusting my cake leveler. After trimming, brush the crumbs off the sponge cakes, as they can make masking very difficult and spoil the filling.

2 Stick a cake board in the center of the cake disk using buttercream or ganache, then place the disk on a nonslip turntable (optional). Spread the cake board with a thin layer of buttercream or ganache and stick the first cake layer on top (brown side downward). Use a pastry brush to soak the top of the sponge with sugar syrup, if required.

3 If the filling is different to that which will be used to coat the outside of the cake, put some of the outer coating mixture in a pastry bag and pipe a ring around the edge of the layer. This will form a barrier to hold the filling inside.

4 Use a palette knife to spread the filling over the bottom layer.

5 Spread out the filling evenly, making sure it goes right to the edges (or meets the ring applied in step 3). Be careful not to use too much filling; if applied too heavily, the filling will ooze out around the sides when the next sponge layer is put in place.

6 Place the next sponge layer on top and add more sugar syrup if required.

7 Repeat steps 3 to 5. If your cake has more than three layers, repeat these steps until you just have the top layer left to add.

8 Position the final layer on top, brown side upward.

9 Once all the layers are assembled, gently press on the top layer to release any trapped air bubbles. Make sure the top is level. Soak the final layer with sugar syrup if required.

MASKING TECHNIQUE

TO ACHIEVE A BEAUTIFULLY MASKED LAYER CAKE, IT IS IMPORTANT TO HAVE THE RIGHT EQUIPMENT (PAGE 8). I ALSO RECOMMEND HAVING A DAMP CLOTH TO HAND, TO CLEAN THE EDGE OF YOUR PALETTE KNIFE AND SIDE SCRAPER AS YOU WORK. YOUR FROSTING SHOULD BE SPREADABLE AND LUMP FREE, AND ENSURE THAT IT IS AT ROOM TEMPERATURE BEFORE USE. YOU WILL NEED TO MASK ANY CAKE TWICE TO ACHIEVE A SMOOTH FINISH AND STRAIGHT EDGES; HOWEVER, YOU CAN REPEAT THE PROCESS UNTIL YOU ARE HAPPY WITH THE RESULT. DO BEAR IN MIND THAT YOU WILL NEED TO CHILL THE CAKE AFTER EACH COAT, TO SET THE FROSTING. USE A SEPARATE BOWL FOR THE CRUMB COAT, TO AVOID SPOILING THE FROSTING FOR THE FINAL COAT.

1 Begin by applying a crumb coat. This will hold the sponge surface in place and provide a good basic shape with which to work. Using a palette knife, pile a generous amount of buttercream or ganache onto the top layer of the cake.

2 Working from the center, spread the mixture toward the edges of the cake and down the sides.

3 As you spread the mixture around the sides, work your palette knife in a backward and forward motion, rotating the turntable in the opposite direction to the way that you're spreading.

4 Ensure that the cake is completely covered and that there are no gaps around the sides.

5 Place the side scraper on the far side of the cake, with the long straight edge against the cake at a 45° angle and the bottom of the side scraper sitting flat on the disk. Place your spare hand on the disk and the turntable, as close to your other hand as possible.

6 Rotate the turntable against the direction of the side scraper, smoothing the frosting until your hands meet at the front.

7 If there are still a lot of cracks or gaps in the frosting, repeat the side-scraping process. Once you are happy with the coating, lift off the side scraper and then clean it with the palette knife.

8 Use a palette knife to make the top of the cake smooth and neaten the edges.

9 Use the side scraper and the palette knife to remove any excess mixture.

Let the cake chill in the refrigerator for at least half an hour, then repeat the crumb coat if necessary, until you are happy with the shape.

Chill the cake again, until it is set.

To apply the final coat, repeat steps 1 to 9 using a fresh, crumb-free batch of buttercream or ganache. Aim for a perfectly level top and straight sides with sharp edges, to achieve the best result.

When you are satisfied with the final coat, put the cake back in the refrigerator for about 1 hour, or until the buttercream or ganache has set. Then apply any finishing touches.

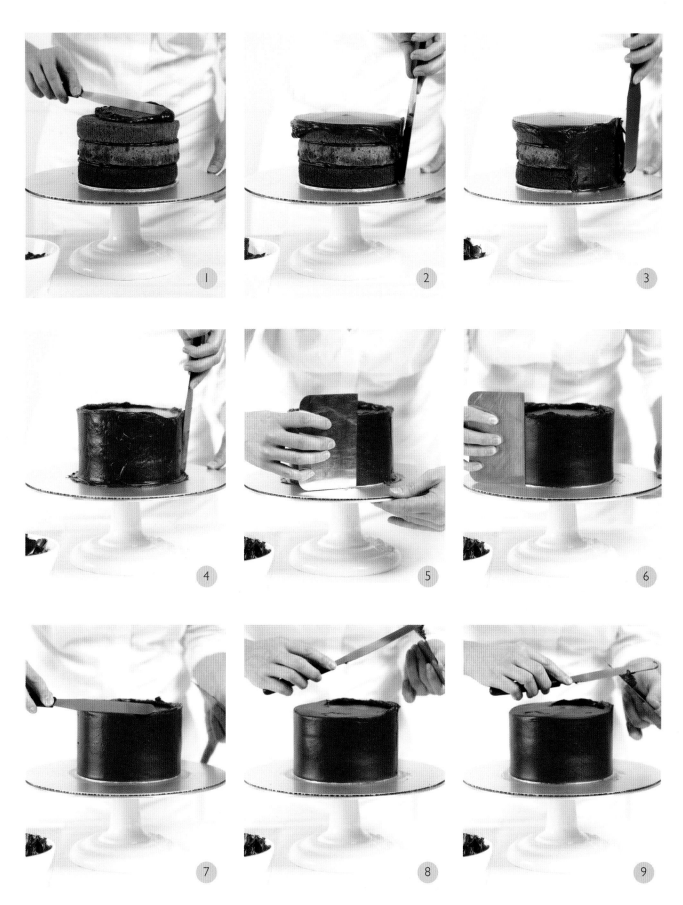

ROUND PIPING
TIP NO. 3

CRIMPED STAR
TIP

LOOP PIPING TECHNIQUE

SMALL LEAF TIP

SWAG PIPING TECHNIQUE

SNAIL TRAIL PIPING TECHNIQUE

HYDRANGEAS AND
LEAF TECHNIQUE

MEDIUM PETAL TIP

ROSE AND LEAF PIPING
TECHNIQUE

BLOSSOM PIPING
TECHNIQUE

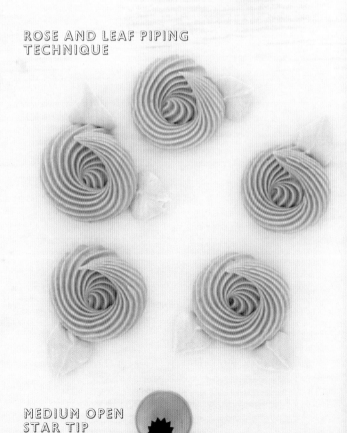

MEDIUM OPEN
STAR TIP

LARGE OPEN STAR
TIP

MEDIUM OPEN
STAR TIP

STAR PIPING
TECHNIQUE

ROSETTE PIPING
TECHNIQUE

ROUND PIPING
TIP NO. 3

MEDIUM
BASKET WEAVE
TIP

ROPE PIPING
TECHNIQUE

OPEN STAR
TIP NO. 7

BASKET WEAVE PIPING
TECHNIQUE

INDEX

A

almond
    peach and almond torte 142–5
    snowball cake 30–3
apple, toffee apple cake 64–7

B

baking tips 9
banana sponge 122–5
berry basket case 96–9, 155
black forest cake 118–21
black and white devil's food cake
    68–71
blossom designs 136–41, 154
blueberry
    berry basket case 96–9
    blueberry and buttermilk cake
        18–21
buttercream, English 10, 92–5,
    126–9, 136–41
    chocolate 17, 117
    cinnamon 104–9
    coffee 86–91
    see also meringue buttercream
buttermilk sponge 18–25

C

cake crumbs 60–3, 68–71
cake pans 9
caramel
caramel cream-cheese frosting
    64–7
    caramel sponge 34–9
    dipping caramel 64–7
    salted caramel cake 34–9
champagne and strawberry cake
    126–9
checkerboard cake, Mad Hatter's
    136–41, 155
cheeky monkey cake 122–5
cherry, black forest cake 118–21
chiffon sponge 40–5, 54–9, 96–9,
    114–17
chocolate
    black forest cake 118–21
    black and white devil's food cake
        68–71

chocolate buttercream 17, 117
chocolate ganache 13, 14–17,
    34–9, 76–81, 114–17, 130–5
chocolate praline truffle cake
    76–81
chocolate sponge 14–17, 34–9,
    118–21, 136–41
    raspberry kiss cake 14–17
    red velvet cake 60–3
    salted caramel cake 34–9
cinnamon
    cinnamon buttercream 104–9
    cinnamon cream-cheese frosting
        110–13
    cinnamon meringue buttercream
        142–5
    cinnamon sponge 104–9
    cinnamon syrup 104–9
    s'mores cake 130–5
    spiced pumpkin cake 110–13
    citrus cake 92–5
coconut
    coconut meringue buttercream
        30–3
    passion fruit and mascarpone
        cake 72–5
    piña colada cake 146–9
coffee
    coffee buttercream 86–91
    coffee sponge 86–91
    coffee syrup 86–91
cookies
    cookie cream-cheese frosting
        46–9
    cookies and cream cake 46–9
cream-cheese frosting 12
    caramel 64–7
    cinnamon 110–13
    cookie 46–9
    honey 22–5
    kirsch 118–21
    lemon 100–3
    lime 146–9
    maple 82–5
    pink-grapefruit 92–5
    vanilla 18–21, 60–3, 68–71
crumb coats 152–3

D

devil's food cake, black and white
    68–71
dragees 126–9

F

floral designs 96–9, 136–41,
    146–9, 154–5
French violet cake 54–9
frosting
    mascarpone 12, 72–5, 86–91
    see also cream-cheese frosting

G

ganache see chocolate ganache
gâteau aux fleur de violettes 54–9
gingerbread cake 100–3
Grand Marnier syrup 142–5

H

hazelnut praline filling 76–81
honey
    honey cream-cheese frosting
        22–5
    honey syrup 22–5, 130–5
    milk and honey cake 22–5
honeycomb 22–5
hydrangea designs 136–41, 154

I

Italian meringue 130–5

J

jam fillings 96–9, 126–9
jelly, passion fruit 72–5

K

kirsch frosting 118–21

L

layering technique 150–1
lemon
    citrus cake 92–5
    lemon, raspberry, and rose cake
        50–3
    lemon cream-cheese frosting
        100–3

lemon sponge 50–3
lemon syrup 50–3
lime
citrus cake 92–5
lime cream-cheese frosting 146–9
piña colada cake 146–9

M

Mad Hatter's checkerboard cake
    136–41, 155
Malibu syrup 146–9
mango mascarpone frosting 72–5
maple and walnut cake 82–5
mascarpone
    mascarpone frosting 12, 72–5,
        86–91
    passion fruit and mascarpone
        cake 72–5
masking technique 152–3
measurements 9
meringue, Italian 130–5
meringue buttercream 10, 14–17,
    76–81, 96–9, 114–17, 130–5
    cinnamon 142–5
    coconut 30–3
    peanut 122–5
    raspberry 50–3
    rose 26–9
    vanilla 40–5
    violet 54–9
milk and honey cake 22–5

N

Neapolitan cake 114–17

O

orange, citrus cake 92–5

P

passion fruit
    passion fruit jelly 72–5
    passion fruit and mascarpone
        cake 72–5
peach and almond torte 142–5
peanut meringue buttercream
    122–5
piña colada cake 146–9

pineapple
    piña colada cake 146–9
    pineapple flowers 146–9
pink-grapefruit frosting 92–5
piping techniques 154–5
pistachio and rose cake 26–9
plum, sugar plum cake 104–9
praline filling 76–81
pumpkin cake, spiced 110–13

R

raspberry
    berry basket case 96–9
    lemon, raspberry, and rose cake
        50–3
    raspberry kiss cake 14–17
    raspberry meringue buttercream
        50–3
red velvet cake 60–3
rose
    lemon, raspberry, and rose cake
        50–3
    rose meringue buttercream
        26–9
    rose and pistachio cake 26–9
rosebud designs 136–41, 154–5

S

salted caramel cake 34–9
s'mores cake 130–5
snowball cake 30–3
spiced cakes
    s'mores cake 130–5
    spiced pumpkin cake 110–13
    toffee apple cake 64–7
stencil work 26–9, 40–5, 54–9
strawberry
    berry basket case 96–9
    strawberry and champagne cake
        126–9
sugar dust 26–9
sugar plum cake 104–9
sugar syrup 13, 26–9, 68–71,
    100–3
    cinnamon 104–9
    citrus 92–5
    coffee 86–91

Grand Marnier 142–5
lemon 50–3
Malibu 146–9
maple 82–5
vanilla 18–21, 30–49, 54–9,
    64–7, 72–5, 96–9, 114–17,
    122–5, 136–41

T

temperatures and timings 9
tiramisu cake 86–91
toffee apple cake 64–7
tool kits 8
torte, peach and almond 142–5
truffle cake, chocolate praline
    76–81

V

vanilla
    vanilla cloud cake 40–5
    vanilla cream-cheese frosting
        18–21, 60–3, 68–71
    vanilla meringue buttercream
        40–5
    vanilla sponge 34–9, 72–5,
        126–9, 136–41
    vanilla syrup 18–21, 30–49,
        54–9, 64–7, 72–5, 96–9,
        114–17, 122–5, 136–41
violet
    French violet cake 54–9
    violet meringue buttercream
        54–9

W

walnut and maple cake 82–5

SUPPLIERS

MOST OF THE EQUIPMENT AND INGREDIENTS USED TO MAKE THE RECIPES IN THIS BOOK ARE WIDELY AVAILABLE FROM SPECIALIST CAKE DECORATING SUPPLIERS AND, INCREASINGLY, THE MORE EVERYDAY ITEMS CAN BE FOUND IN GROCERY STORES AND GENERAL COOKWARE STORES. HOWEVER, TO OFFER SOME GUIDANCE, AND TO HELP YOU TO FIND THE MORE SPECIALIST ITEMS, I HAVE LISTED SOME USEFUL WEBSITES BELOW.

My own website includes an online store where you can purchase specialist cake decorating tools and ingredients as well as an assortment of shallow sandwich pans, cake stencils, and other bakeware products. In addition, there is a small selection of cake fillings:

Peggy Porschen Cakes
www.peggyporschen.com

For cake pans:
Silverwood Quality Bakeware
www.alansilverwood.com

For cake stencils, silicon molds (such as the insect mold for the Milk and Honey Cake on page 22, made by First Impressions), food colors, and general baking and cake decorating equipment:
The Cake Decorating Co.
www.thecakedecoratingcompany.co.uk

For turntables:
Ateco
www.globalsugarart.com

Knightsbridge PME
www.cakedecoration.co.uk

For piping tips and patterned side scrapers:
Wilton
www.wilton.com

For specialist ingredients:
Whole Foods Market
www.wholefoodsmarket.com

Throughout each year, I run a series of baking and cake-decorating classes at the Peggy Porschen Academy. So whether you want to perfect your piping techniques to create irresistible cakes or brush up your baking skills to make heavenly cupcakes, there is a suitable course:

Peggy Porschen Academy
30 Elizabeth Street
Belgravia
London SW1W 9RB
www.peggyporschen.com

Each morning my team of specialist bakers freshly bake a range of layer cakes, cupcakes, cookies, and other yummy delights for visitors to the Peggy Porschen Parlour to either enjoy there and then with an artisan tea blend or coffee or to take away for a teatime treat. If you have enjoyed the recipes in this book, I hope you will pay us a visit:

Peggy Porschen Parlour
116 Ebury Street
Belgravia
London SW1W 9QQ
www.peggyporschen.com

ACKNOWLEDGMENTS

Lovely Layer Cakes has been a labor of true love. An enormous amount of research, test baking, writing, photographing, and more went into this book. I couldn't have done it without the help of a wonderful team of some very dedicated, talented people.

My first thank you goes to my long-term publisher Quadrille, with whom I have been working now for 10 fantastic years. I would especially like to thank Jane O'Shea, my publishing director. Thank you for "discovering" me, for giving me all these amazing opportunities, and for having shared my creative vision right from the start. I will miss working with you. To the other lovely ladies at Quadrille—Lisa Pendreigh, Helen Lewis, and Gemma Hayden—thank you for everything and working so hard with me to add another beautiful title to the collection.

To my photographer, the one and only Georgia Glynn Smith, who goes above and beyond and produces the most beautiful pictures, every time. And to her assistant, Bobby—a huge, huge thank you to you both; it's been so much fun working with you at the shoots. Thank you to my lovely stylist Rebecca Newport, for all the beautiful props and setting the scene.

Probably the greatest thanks I owe to my fantastic staff member Michele Stander. Thank you so much for all your amazing help with the recipe testing and writing. You have put so much enthusiasm, talent, and hard work into this book. You have made an incredible contribution and the result is a wonderful collection of deliciousness. I am very proud to have you in my team.

To Stephanie Maughan, thank you for your fantastic support, brainstorming ideas, and help putting the concept together. Alexia Terzopulou, thank you for your editorial work. Another big thank you goes to the rest of my team at the Peggy Porschen Group. Whenever I am writing a book, it means a lot of extra work for everyone and disruption to their normal working day. I thank you guys for all your support and for keeping things going while Michele and I were producing this book.

Thank you to my neighbors and foodie friends Brian, Anke, and Nicholas Ma Siy for tasting all our test cakes and giving your valuable feedback. I am so sorry for making you eat that much cake.

And to the most important people in my life, my little family. Bryn and Max, I love you both so, so much. My baby boy, Max, you made me so proud modeling for the Cheeky Monkey Cake.